Praise for the Pareto System,
Featured in *Breakthrough Business Development*

"I wholeheartedly recommend the Pareto System to anyone who seeks to improve their business and position themselves as the advisor of choice. The Pareto System helped me get results by systematically taking my practice apart and putting it back together in a way that created, and will continue to create, raving fans. Furthermore, I have been able to systematize my practice, which has created more time for me and my family. The service provided was excellent. The program is of great value and was totally worth my investment."

Victoria, British Columbia

"The personal coaching of the Pareto System has given me a very effective client-centered process. This system has vastly improved my professionalism, my presentation skills and my client delivery. I believe Pareto has enhanced my ability to (1) develop and maintain a long-term, trusting relationship with my clients, and (2) grow my practice with an improved quality of clientele. More importantly, this system holds us accountable to follow a process that facilitates the realization of clients' goals."

Chicago, Illinois

"Our service levels have made a *huge* difference in the level of our client satisfaction. It has helped to increase client loyalty because clients know what to expect from us now and they also are more comfortable referring us to friends, etc. For example, we have had a client for several years and we did not know her at all. Since we met with her and completed the Personal Financial Policy Statement (provided by Pareto), she has transferred in over a million in assets and she could not be more appreciative of our efforts. She has quickly become one of our favorite clients and she is singing our praises and trying to find us a suitable introduction."

New York, New York

"Pareto has revolutionized my business. They have given me a much greater understanding of the elements of a successful practice. They have assisted me in implementing these elements effectively, particularly in those areas where my existing attitudes and fears got in the way. The coaching program made all the difference. I strongly recommend Pareto to anyone who wants to feel that they are running their business and it is not running them…Thanks for the help!"

Edmonton, Alberta

"I've received such a positive response from our event held last Thursday that I'm beginning to wonder how I will top it next year! Your presentation was most certainly a highlight of the day for everyone in attendance. After listening for two hours, I'm sure there was not one [who] could claim leaving without a new idea or simply a new-found enthusiasm to put to use in their business."

Denver, Colorado

"We have been using the Pareto Systems program for the past three months. Although we have not completed the entire program (we're about two-thirds through), we have already seen significant improvements in our business in this short time. Since we've started the program, we were referred and have transferred in both a $2,500,000 client and a $1,000,000 client. We're also in the process of meeting with and transferring in several more qualified referrals. Of course all of the new assets are a great benefit; however, the most important benefit of going through this program is making our business run a lot more efficiently in the long term. We are already seeing that our time is used more efficiently in the office (we still have room to improve on this) and that our clients are enjoying a significantly higher level of service and consistency. If two people of very average intelligence and charm (my partner and me) can make this work, most advisors certainly could very well do the same. Thanks again for your great follow-up and tremendous support!"

San Diego, California

"From a Wholesaler's standpoint I couldn't imagine running my business without a process in place like Pareto's. The ability to focus my attention and have procedures in place has allowed me to put a foundation in my business that gives me ample room to grow. Thanks again!"

Carmel, Indiana

"I'd like to thank everyone at Pareto for a great consulting experience. I'm no stranger to coaching…but I have to say that the Pareto System is the most practical and useful coaching program I have seen or experienced. In particular, the concept of systematizing client and office processes to ensure a consistent, world-class experience is very powerful. It's an idea that's intuitive but much more easily said than done. I think you have made 'doing it' as easy as it's going to get! Thanks again."

Gold River, California

"I began working with Pareto Systems one year ago. The immediate impact on my business was tremendous. By the end of the year, I had experienced my best production month, and I had established myself solidly with a number of new clients. The Pareto System has been of inestimable assistance to me during difficult times [when] my goal became one of keeping existing clients. Incorporating the principles of the Pareto System has resulted not only in client decisions to stay with me, but to also bring additional assets to their accounts here. The Pareto System is a unique program…Thank you."

Hampton, Virginia

"Dear Pareto, There is no question that your system is the finest I have ever used. I feel as if I have taken the first steps up Mount Everest. My team and I also want to discuss the possibility of having the full treatment (customized consulting) sometime in the not-so-distant future. Thanks for all the updates."

St. Louis, Missouri

SINCE 1957

Dynamic Funds™

Invest with Advice.

Dear Advisor,

Dynamic's core belief in the value of professional financial advice guides everything we do. Through every step of our development over the past 50 years, we have supported this belief, knowing that expert, impartial advice is crucial in helping investors achieve long-term financial security.

Through our sponsorship of this business-building book, Dynamic Funds is pleased to support you in taking your business to the next level.

When you, Canada's financial advisors, are supported in learning and implementing more efficient processes and strategies within your businesses, you can devote more time and effort to your true profession: helping Canadians accumulate wealth, protect wealth, use wealth and enjoy wealth.

The proven strategies in this book and the helpful templates on the related website will help you become more efficient and effective in running your business. As a result, you will increase your capacity to help more Canadians to "Invest with Advice."

Sincerely,

Jordy Chilcott
Senior Vice-President and
National Sales Manager
Dynamic Funds
advisor.dynamic.ca

BREAKTHROUGH BUSINESS DEVELOPMENT

A 90-DAY PLAN TO BUILD YOUR CLIENT BASE AND TAKE YOUR BUSINESS TO THE NEXT LEVEL

Duncan MacPherson and David Miller

John Wiley & Sons Canada, Ltd.

Library and Archives Canada Cataloguing in Publication Data

MacPherson, Duncan, 1965-
    Breakthrough business development : a 90-day plan to build your client base and take your business to the next level / Duncan MacPherson, David Miller.

Includes index.
ISBN 978-0-470-84096-2

    1. Marketing—Management. 2. Sales. 3. Business planning.
4. Knowledge management. 5. Success in business. I. Title.

HD30.28.M335 2007   658.8   C2007-903701-1

Production Credits
Cover design: Jason Vandenberg
Interior text design: Tegan Wallace
Wiley Bicentennial Logo: Richard J. Pacifico
Printer: Quebecor - Taunton

John Wiley & Sons Canada, Ltd.
6045 Freemont Blvd.
Mississauga, Ontario
L5R 4J3

Printed and bound in the United States of America

1 2 3 4 5 QW 11 10 09 08 07

To our families

TABLE OF CONTENTS

PREFACE

After a successful multi-year strategic alliance between our two original firms, Duncan MacPherson & Associates and Mindset International, we decided to formally combine our strengths by establishing Pareto Systems in 2000.

We called our company Pareto Systems because of our fascination with the many layers of the Pareto Principle and how they impact an entrepreneur. Also known as the eighty-twenty rule, the Pareto Principle suggests, for starters, that approximately eighty percent of an entrepreneur's business is generated by about twenty percent of his or her clients. Our objective has always been to help entrepreneurs predictably attract and keep clients like those in the twentieth percentile while creating a precise and efficient business in the process.

Because of our fixation on predictable execution and quantifiable results, our business development and practice management coaching and consulting services grew steadily. In 2003, we unveiled the Pareto Platform, a one-of-a-kind business-building solution that integrates time-tested best practices with a turnkey, Web-based Client Relationship Management (CRM) system. Today, entrepreneurs and their teams from a variety of sectors in the marketplace use the Platform every day to consistently manage and maximize their client relationships while deploying our tried-and-true concepts and procedures. We haven't looked back since.

It's funny how the word "entrepreneur" conjures up different meanings for different people. Some people think it's a French word for someone who works at home in their underwear (that would make for a strange Casual Friday if you think about it). Others think it describes someone who can't hold a real job or is a dreamer or serial opportunity-chaser. In truth, an entrepreneur is someone who likes autonomy and has a vision for how to bring value to clients. They are hard-working, persuasive, dedicated, motivated and resilient. Rather than simply *have* a job and *make* some money, they want to build something that is *worth* a lot of money while maximizing their personal fulfillment.

As you are about to read, we are going to walk you through our process, which will enable you to take your business to the next level and ultimately experience a breakthrough. Like any book on this topic, there are countless ideas to be found in these pages. Unlike a lot of books on this topic, you can rest assured that everything we suggest has been proven to work. Not a single concept is theoretical or on trial. Everything has been time-tested by ourselves in our own business and by the coaching and consulting clients who have hired us over the years. The success stories we've seen first-hand from our clients have often been staggering. In one recent example, an already extremely successful new client decided to simply implement our process to attract referrals from his clients. After three months of refinement and mastery, this client generated more new business in one month of actual implementation than in the entire previous year!

But it doesn't stop there. While most authors tell you *why* you should be using their ideas and concepts and sprinkle in the occasional hero story like the one we just gave you, we won't leave you hanging like that—we'll also show you *how* to implement our ideas. After all, you read a book to get better results, not just ideas, right?

On our website, **www.paretoplatform.com**, you will find the seventeen turnkey, actionable templates for the core ideas we describe in this book. You and your team can download these proven strategies for free and implement them to translate these concepts into results. Furthermore, you can register to receive updates and visit our blog, which we update on a regular basis. Check **www.breakthroughbusinessdevelopment.com** often to get up-to-the-minute insights.

At the risk of belaboring the point, a lot of people tell us that they like our ideas and creativity. We aren't creative. Any appearance of creativity stems from our ability to simply conceal our sources.

All kidding aside, the feedback and results achieved by our clients over the years act as an ongoing stress-testing mechanism that you can rely on. So strive to implement the ideas you like, ASAP! We say that because we believe the value of reading a book begins when you are finished reading it. If you can execute the relevant concepts quickly and quantify the impact, well then, reading this book will have been a good investment. Just don't delay. You've heard the old saying, "After all is said and done, more is often said than done." Don't let the Law of Diminishing Intent rob you of the value of what's in here.

Duncan and David

ACKNOWLEDGMENTS

We have many people to thank for helping this book become a reality.

To our many clients over the years—both individual and corporate—we've learned as much or more from you as you have from us. Your efforts and contributions are greatly appreciated.

To our head of consulting at Pareto Systems, Tom Frisby, thanks for your tireless commitment and unwavering loyalty. You and your team have helped take our business to the next level.

To our head of technology at Pareto Platform, Darren Hennessey, thanks for your outstanding vision and execution and your never-ending commitment to continual refinement. Our clients run better businesses and lead better lives thanks to you and your team.

To our entire team of consulting, technology and support staff, your dedication has been invaluable and has enabled us to focus on crucial business development projects such as this.

To our various mentors and to all the practice management and business development gurus we've worked with—especially Mr. Jim Rohn—thank you for your important contributions. Our business acumen and our personal lives are richer because of your countless insights.

We'd also like to thank the exceptional crew at John Wiley & Sons, our publisher. Your professionalism and support have helped make this project a pleasure to undertake.

And finally, we would like to thank our wives and children. If ever the expression "Behind every successful man is a shocked and amazed woman" applied, it would be with us. And we'd be remiss if we didn't say we are both incredibly proud fathers of great kids.

INTRODUCTION

OVERVIEW OF OUR STAR BUSINESS PLANNING PROCESS

Throughout this book, we will walk you through the exact process we use with our coaching and consulting clients, as well as within our Pareto Platform, framed by our business development acronym STAR. Our hope is that you will create a personalized business development plan using our methodology.

Achieving a breakthrough is done by design, not by luck or chance. It starts when you gain clarity about how you should move forward and what opportunities you should act on. A solid plan will kick-start that process. Within our coaching and consulting process, as well as with our Platform subscribers, we are constantly urging entrepreneurs to create and rely on a business development plan.

This book has been written, along with the actionable templates on our website, to urge you to do the same.

The purpose of sculpting a plan is to enable you to stop for a moment to kick your own tires and conduct a personalized state-of-the-nation regarding your business. Think things through, effectively analyze your business, and then crystallize your thoughts on paper to create a guidance system going forward. The process in and of itself is powerful and revealing. Furthermore, you then have a blueprint to guide you as you embark on your business development journey. We use STAR because we feel it represents what we like to think of as the four cornerstones of a good, solid plan. We are convinced that, like the sun shining through a magnifying glass, with this plan you can harness and focus the power that you already possess and make tangible progress quickly.

Think of STAR as if it is a combination lock. Each of these letters represents a number in the combination. If you dial all the numbers in the combination in the right sequence, good things will happen.

The S in STAR is the *strategic analysis*. It may sound trite, but it is crucial that you continually analyze your business. If you think about where you are today and where you want to be in the next twelve months, the space between those two places, between today and next year, is called *the gap*. It is important to conduct a gap analysis, as this process will enable you to analyze what needs to occur in your business to take you to that next level and achieve a breakthrough. Whether you're currently humming along, have hit a plateau or have simply run out of gas or new ideas, this process can be invaluable to you.

The T stands for *targets and goals*. After the strategic analysis process, proceed to goal-setting and examine where you see yourself in the future. This process will build anticipation and provide enduring motivation as you move forward.

The heavy work begins with the A in STAR—*activities!* These are the actions you'll engage in to achieve your desired results. Based on the Law of Cause and Effect, you'll identify the activities you should deploy on an ongoing basis in order to meet the productivity goals you've set.

The R is the *reality check*. This simple process will hold you accountable as you go forward.

As you go through this process, you may come to one of the following three realizations:

1. I'm actually doing okay. This is a good validation.

2. I'm on the verge of a breakthrough and this is going to tip me over to a whole new level.

3. I can't believe how much I'm doing wrong! This book has revealed some majors flaws in my approach.

Either way, if you feel you need to make some dramatic adjustments, minor adjustments or simply stick to the course you're on, this book will be of value to you. Some of our clients in the past have been pleasantly surprised because they were at the proverbial tipping point with their business and just needed a nudge from us to break through to the next level. For others, we confirmed their suspicions that they had some big issues in terms of staff accountability, systems, and client loyalty, to name a few areas. We've seen the full spectrum of issues out there and are confident that virtually all of them can be addressed using this process.

We must say that while there are numerous universal issues addressed in this book that affect virtually all entrepreneurs, our mindset and philosophy is especially effective for knowledge-for-profit business professionals and those who focus on long-term client relationships. That's not to say this book won't be of benefit to entrepreneurs who are more transactional. Many points are in fact applicable even if you happen to sell your services or solutions to a customer once with only limited potential for repeat business. (The timeshare salesperson or the injury lawyer you see on late night TV ads or on the back cover of your yellow pages are good examples.) However, if you "think for a living," as in some of the professions listed below, and if you view client relationships as an actual asset because of their ongoing needs and potential flag-waving opportunities, we can say with certainty that these concepts and processes will serve you well:

- financial advisor
- accountant
- lawyer
- insurance broker
- consultant
- architect
- engineer
- contractor
- wholesaler
- medical professional
- mortgage broker
- real estate specialist

That said, not everything in the format we present it in will be appropriate for all readers. Nor are we suggesting that this will address every issue and episode that matters in entrepreneurship. Far from it. Again, while we're confident that we'll trigger a few "eureka moments" as you read this, what we are really hoping you'll do is select the concepts that are appropriate for you and customize them to suit your own style and situation.

One last point. Do not be misled by the apparent simplicity of some of the concepts we discuss. We live in an era where people are looking for a dramatic idea or a silver bullet. Too often, an idea gets ignored if it isn't fancy or esoteric or if it sounds familiar. Yes, a lot of these ideas are common sense. Here is the question to consider, however: Is common sense a common practice within your business? If we may be so bold, we're going to ask you to "hold up the mirror" and ask yourself if your current knowledge of what *should* be done is an actual reflection of what *is* getting done on a day-to-day basis. Please don't rule out an idea because you've heard it before. We've laid out these concepts in a methodical and sequential manner designed for implementation. Give them a chance to work for you. To paraphrase the old saying, "The lessons are simple; it's the student who is complicated." At the risk of sounding preachy, we say: keep it simple.

We have seen countless examples of downright basic concepts executed flawlessly that consequently generate staggering results. For example, a while back we urged our clients to send their clients Thanksgiving Cards in autumn rather than holiday cards in December. Our logic was simple: Virtually everyone sends holiday cards in December and often it seems like the senders are just going through the motions. The Thanksgiving cards are unique and they stand out. Countless clients have made this minor adjustment and realized major benefits as a result.

As we mentioned, this book has been written in a sequential way that will enable you to enhance your momentum and build the bridge to improved results as you cross it. All seventeen templates on our website can be implemented within the next twelve weeks and, in the process, should help you achieve a breakthrough. Again, based on our experience, this slow and steady implementing of linked and sequential ideas together over time is predictable. Think about improving your golf game or trying to learn a new language. What do you feel would be more effective, attending a weekend boot camp or retreat and being bombarded with information, or being exposed to smaller portions weekly over an extended period of time? Your retention and ability to achieve mastery is far more likely when you break things down and chip away at them over time.

On behalf of everyone on our team, we wish you great success as you move ahead with this. We'd love to hear from you, so visit our website and drop us a line sometime.

PART 1:
STRATEGIC ANALYSIS
(WEEKS 1–4)

CHAPTER 1
YOUR UNTAPPED OPPORTUNITIES

Order is a temporary illusion. Strategy is a moving target.

Rosabeth Moss Cantor

The first part of this book is designed to urge you to step back and reflect on how you have shaped your business up until now. We've all done a lot of things right over the years and we've all made a few mistakes here and there. Well, going forward, the goal is to try not to repeat those errors in judgment, while building on our momentum.

This personal assessment will reveal even minor adjustments that could and should be made in order to improve your effectiveness. Often, these minor adjustments can lead to major improvements. There's a law in business called the Law of Optimization (you'll soon realize we really like universal laws of business and life), which states that no matter how well an approach or process works, it can always be refined and improved upon, even if those refinements and improvements are very subtle.

This approach is especially important for entrepreneurs because we have a tendency to operate in a vacuum with very little input or support from others. Entrepreneurs are independent by nature and can unconsciously drift onto a track that isn't as efficient as it could be. Too often, we've met business owners with ten years of experience who in fact really had one year of experience ten times over. They were in a loop, a pattern of simply repeating their approaches with little refinement. Yes, this can achieve results, but there is a fine line between being in a groove and being in a rut.

The strategic analysis also reminds us of the importance of being realistic. Peter Drucker, legendary management authority and elder statesman of quality in business, said, "As an entrepreneur you have to deal with things as they are, not as you wish they were." We can relate. The vast majority of entrepreneurs we know are incredibly optimistic and even sometimes optimistic to a fault, to the point where it actually negatively affects their judgment. We understand because we are also entrepreneurs and even we don't always deal with today's realities. Instead, we might subconsciously focus on how good things will be in the future and overlook certain realities that need to be addressed right now. As Aldous Huxley said, "Facts don't cease to exist because they are ignored."

Yes, we absolutely must be optimistic to run our own businesses. The Reality Principle simply reminds us we can't always trust our own judgment or believe our own hype. To be objective we have to be brutally honest with ourselves and have a process that forces us out of our vacuum. (As Canadians, we know all about optimism. Why else would we spend $30 on a snow shovel and $500 on a lawn mower?)

IDENTIFY AND TAKE ADVANTAGE

In the spirit of striving to achieve clarity, one of the first things you want to do as part of the strategic analysis is strive to identify untapped opportunities in your business. Every entrepreneur we've ever met, to varying degrees, was sitting on a virtual gold mine of untapped opportunity. Most don't even realize it. *Acres of Diamonds,* a great little book by Russell Conwell, tells a story about an ambitious farmer who got a little bored and wanted to go out into the world to find his pot of gold. He sold his farm to raise some money and away he went. He ended up dying a pauper. Meanwhile, the farm he sold turned out to be loaded with diamonds. Admittedly that is a little dramatic but we see entrepreneurs—again, to varying degrees—sitting on those acres of unrealized wealth. One of the most tangibly rewarding aspects of the solutions we provide is helping business owners identify their own untapped potential. The next few pages will hopefully help you discover the same.

Remember

> » Sound judgment leads to good decisions.
> » Apply the Law of Optimization and the Reality Principle as you analyze your business.

Take Action Now! (Week 1)

> » Download the STAR Business Planning Tool found on our website, **www.paretoplatform.com**, to begin the process of gaining clarity for your own untapped opportunities and overlooked vulnerabilities.
> » Visit **www.breakthroughbusinessdevelopment.com** to see insights and stories from the field on this topic and others.

CHAPTER 2
MARKETING PILLARS AND THE LOYALTY LADDER

It's more important to reach people who count than it is to count the number of people you are reaching.

Marketing Maxim

In keeping with striving to identify your untapped opportunities, your next step is to establish what we refer to as your marketing pillars. When we sit down with an entrepreneur and scrutinize his or her business, one of the first things we'll do is draw three vertical lines on a sheet of paper. Each line is a pillar representing an existing or prospective target marketing opportunity. We call them pillars because, in a perfect world, you want a business built on a strong foundation that creates multiple income streams—steady streams of predictable, sustainable business.

Let's define each of the fundamental pillars that can be created for virtually any business. The first and most important pillar, and this should be self-evident, is made up of your *existing client relation-ships*—especially the twenty percent who generate eighty percent of your business. They are the most valuable asset you'll ever possess. Your client relationships are proprietary and often take years to nurture and maximize in terms of their potential. Yet too many entrepreneurs strive to pursue new clients using flawed and expensive prospecting tactics and, in the process, take existing clients for granted and leave them twisting in the wind. As you'll see in a moment, this becomes a huge untapped opportunity.

The second pillar represents *promotional partners*. These are strategic alliances—the people in the marketplace with whom you collaborate to achieve a mutually beneficial outcome.

The third pillar represents your *prospective target markets* based on geographic, demographic and/or socio-economic opportunities available to you.

Later in the book, we'll be expanding on your second and third pillars, but for now let's zero in on your most important untapped opportunity—your existing client relationships. Obviously we don't know how many clients you have right now and frankly it doesn't really matter. What does matter, however, is that your existing clients represent what we call your *inner circle*. And as we said, your inner circle of clients is the most valuable asset you'll ever possess.

A powerful and immutable marketing rule referred to as the Rule of Fifty-Two supports this point. It states that every single client you have right now in your inner circle has their own personal inner circle of approximately fifty-two friends, family members and business associates. Some have more, some have less, but again that's not the point. Do the math, though. If you have, for example, five hundred clients, multiply five hundred times fifty-two. How much opportunity do you have there? A lot. Enough new prospective clients to keep you entertained for three lifetimes.

Said another way, clients are not an "end," but a means to an end, meaning they can be a springboard to tremendous amounts of new business over time. Simply bringing on a new client is no reason to celebrate. If you gain access to each client's friends and acquaintances and maximize each relationship, then you have an exciting business.

IDENTIFY YOUR MVPs

This brings us to our next point—understanding who your Most Valuable Prospects (MVPs) are. Most entrepreneurs think their MVPs are new people in their respective city or market area, when in fact they are the friends and family members of their existing clients. Is it possible that one of your most significant untapped opportunities is a result of your inability to capitalize on each of your existing client relationships vis-à-vis repeat or ongoing business and referrals?

Based on the fact that your clients will have significantly more persuasive impact on their friends and family than you ever will, you need a process to transform your clients into a sales team that will wave your flag. This will ensure that the moment a conversation between your client and any of his or her fifty-two (plus or minus) friends, associates or family members turns to what you do for them, your client will brag about you. That said, are you satisfied with the degree of referability and the quality and quantity of endorsements you are currently attracting?

If you get nothing else from this book, we hope you get this—it is the core of our marketing and business development philosophy. We are referring to the *Loyalty Ladder*. We didn't invent this concept. It's been around for a long time. We've simply adjusted it for clarity as it relates to entrepreneurs specifically. And we are convinced that it will be tremendously helpful to you.

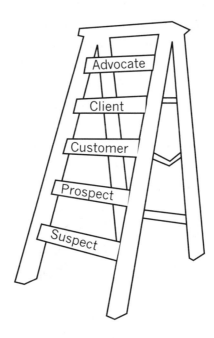

As you can see, the Loyalty Ladder has five rungs and every single person in your market area is on one of those five rungs. You are striving to achieve something called conversion. Your objective is to convert as many people as possible all the way through to the top of the ladder. Let's start at the bottom.

The bottom rung on the ladder is for *suspects*. A suspect is, frankly, anybody with a pulse. Anyone who can fog a mirror is a suspect. Will a business owner receive a good return on his or her investment of time, money, energy and lung capacity from talking to suspects? Clearly not. But we see people all the time who mistake movement for achievement. Or, as Hemingway said, "mistake motion for action." These people are very busy stirring the proverbial pot. But they've yet to figure out the distinction between suspects and the next rung on the ladder, *prospects*.

The difference between a suspect and a prospect is profound and we can sum up the difference with one word, a word worth an MBA in marketing: *pre-disposition*. It's another way of saying *self-motivated*. A prospect is somebody who has been motivated in advance of you ever talking to them. You want your prospects to be motivated but you can't want it more than they do. Wouldn't it be great if every prospect you ever talked to already "wanted it," meaning they were already self-motivated? Motivating people is draining; it can be like pumping air into a leaky tire. True prospects are self-motivated. They are your MVPs.

Your objective is to sift the prospects out of the mass of suspects and, most important, give them a reason to contact you. It's not unlike mining for gold. You have to sift a lot of dirt to find an ounce of gold but you're not trying to turn dirt into gold. With prospects, you're trying to find them, not create them. You're trying to attract them, not chase them. This is what truly defines a prospect. They contact you or a client of yours calls you on their friend's behalf.

Does it get any better than when *your* phone rings? You pick it up and it's one of your favorite clients calling you saying, "Look, I know you're busy and I don't even know if you're accepting new clients right now, but you've got to talk to my buddy." Or maybe a complete stranger calls you up and says, "I was talking to my friend over the weekend and she told me I have to talk to you." Your goal is to increase the frequency of this type of inbound call.

THE LAW OF ATTRACTION

This Law, like most of them, has several layers. From a business development perspective it simply means that there are two ways to get new clients: Chase them or attract them. Which of the two do you feel would be more fulfilling over the long haul? One of our goals is to help you attract, for lack of a better term, more attractive clients to your business. Interestingly enough, your clients will be instrumental in helping you draw a steady stream of quality inbound calls to your business.

It is for this reason that we are not big fans of cold-calling, the rawest form of out-bounding. You might be saddened to know we're not going to suggest you engage in cold-calling. Some people like it. Some people defend it and say, "What are you talking about? It's a great way to build a business." Sure. You can also cut down a tree with a hammer if you try hard enough or keep at it long enough.

Any expenditure of effort will garner a return on investment, but we would prefer that you to maximize your return by employing the Law of Attraction so that you can make your phone ring consistently. We'll expand on this for you when we outline our prospecting process and when we reveal our referral process later on in the book. For now, let's get back to the Loyalty Ladder.

Once you've got your true prospects, your MVPs, in sight, your next job is to convert those prospects into *customers*. At the very least, you want them as customers. You may wonder what we mean by saying *"at the very least."* A profound difference exists between a customer and the next rung on the ladder—a *client*.

Some people use these terms—*client* and *customer*—interchangeably and to them it may all be semantics, but we're going to explain our definition, which will hold true throughout this book. *Clients* are exclusive to you. They empower you fully. Every single thing they need that you provide, they empower you to deliver. Those are *clients*. *Customers*, on the other hand, do some business with you, but they also do business with one or more of your competitors. Customers buy something; clients buy *into* something. Based on that, is there a chance that some of your clients are really only customers? Talk about an untapped opportunity!

Do you currently have a compelling way to convey your full array of offerings in order to convert customers into clients? Is it possible that you have some customers currently who aren't aware of all the services you provide? And can you position the concept of full empowerment as a service to your customers rather than as a benefit to you? In the Activities section of this book we reveal to you the exact proven process our coaching and consulting clients and Pareto Platform subscribers use to gain full empowerment from all their clients.

ADVOCATES: THE ULTIMATE CLIENTS

The last and most important rung on the Loyalty Ladder is reserved for **advocates**. Most entrepreneurs fixate on how many clients they can get, when in fact there is a profound distinction between a client and an advocate.

Clients empower you fully but never send referrals, while advocates are people who think you walk on water. They feel great about your relationship; they trust you and are fiercely loyal. They wouldn't dream of doing business with anybody else. They are fully empowering. Best of all, they brag about you to anybody who'll listen.

The goal isn't to see how many clients you can get, but how many advocates you can get. That's where the value is. Some people talk about how many clients they have and they wear that number like a badge of honor. Think about the advocates you have now. Perhaps you have five or ten. Based on the Rule of Fifty-Two, what would happen to your business if you had 150 advocates? It's not uncommon that when we meet with an entrepreneur and they tell us they have five hundred clients, we find in short order that they really have in the neighborhood of 150 customers, 330 clients and around 20 advocates. Talk about a huge untapped opportunity.

MOVING UP THE LADDER

There is a practical component to the Loyalty Ladder as well as an element of personal fulfillment. It takes far more time, money, effort and energy to convert a new prospect into a customer or client than it does to convert an existing client into a referral-generating advocate. That's a practical fact. But, even more important, every year you are in business should be more fulfilling. The easiest way to achieve this is to stop trying to convince new people and instead work with people who are already convinced. Show them why, who and how they should be introducing people to you. There is an old saying that advises business people to always keep pulling the same way people are already pushing.

To that end, our proven referral process will enable you to coach your advocates as to *why* they should introduce people to you (and address why they aren't referring), *who* they should introduce to you, and *how* they should introduce people to you. And best of all, this process positions referrals as a benefit to your advocates rather than as a favor to you. And that is extremely attractive to high-caliber individuals. Remember, high-net-worth clients don't want to be sold! They appreciate stewardship over salesmanship.

We're asking you to focus on the commitment of advocates rather than simply the commissions or income you earn from new clients. Stop trading your time for money by dwelling on transactions. Focus instead on the lifetime value of relationships with advocates. Relationships can last long after you've spent the money you've earned.

We mentioned that we are going to reveal our referral process in the Actions section of the book, but for now let's get the wheels turning relating to the mindset of refer-ability. Earlier, we asked you to consider *why*, *who* and *how*. If we want more referrals, let's focus first on the *why*. Why don't your clients refer the desired quality and quantity of endorsements your way? Why should they? The *why* speaks to purpose and the *how* speaks to process. Most business-people don't spend much time considering the why, they simply want to know how. But in our experience we can safely say that when it comes to increasing the quality and quantity of referrals you receive, your purpose is just as important as your process. In other words, when the *why* is clear, the *how* gets easy.

POSITION ADVOCACY AS A BENEFIT TO CLIENTS, NOT TO YOU

So again, *why* should a client refer a friend to you? *Why* don't you get as many referrals as you'd like? The answer is probably rooted in how you position referrals.

When you talk to a client about the concept of referrals, do you position it as a service to your clients, or as a favor to yourself? Most people, without really intending to, position referrals as a favor or benefit to themselves. They say things like, "I'm trying to grow my business" or "I'm always looking for new clients" or "I get paid in three ways." The problem with doing this is that you end up looking needy.

We advise you to never bring your needs to your clients. It's not attractive. The "favor" approach can stimulate occasional referrals, but we feel it actually hurts you more than it helps you over the long run. Remember, it's not what you say but rather *what they hear* that really counts. When you ask for a referral because it will help you build your business, what does your client really hear? It creates an atmosphere of obligation rather than pure reciprocation and value.

In fact, if there is anything we want you to convey to your clients it's this: "I don't need the money." Not literally, of course. We mean in terms of a subtle, unspoken theme that is embedded in your approach. By positioning the concept of you making yourself available to help friends of clients, you are really demonstrating the personal fulfillment that comes from helping people make informed decisions. It feels better from your perspective and it is valued and appreciated by your clients.

Take the position, and be sure to absolutely convince yourself, that it's a service you provide. How much more attractive is it to say,

> As a value-added service to my clients, I make myself available to act as a sounding board. You might have a friend who asks you about me, or you might feel compelled to make an introduction to help someone out. If that happens I will make the time to offer objective advice that they can use to make an informed decision. It's a value-added service that I offer to my best clients.

As opposed to saying,

> You are a great client and I'm always looking for more clients just like you because I'm trying to grow my business. Do you know anyone who might need what I sell?

In the Activities section we will disclose this process in its entirety.

Wouldn't it be great if your clients not only knew *why* they should refer someone to you but also *who* is a good fit for you? And who you are good fit for? Do your clients think of you as a specialist who is all things to some people, or do they think of you as a generalist who tries to be all things to all people? In other words, do they know who they should be referring to you? Here is a good qualifier. Have you ever received a referral from a client and, after you met their friend, you dreaded the idea of bringing them on as a new client but did so anyway because you didn't want to offend the client who sent the referral in the first place?

Our process will help you communicate to your clients *who* they should be steering to you. We'll come back to this "quality over quantity" mindset continually.

As promised, our referral approach will also help you provide your clients with a clear and precise process for *how* to actually make an introduction. We don't mean to leave you hanging, but the process we're referring to has been proven to work by our coaching and consulting clients over the last several years and will be provided to you in a turnkey fashion in the Activities section of the book. And of course, all of the scripting and templates you can download from our website are also drawn directly from our coaching curriculum.

Remember

» Empowerment and endorsements by clients must be positioned as a service to them rather than as a favor or benefit to you.

Take Action Now! (Week 1)

» Apply the Loyalty Ladder to your business and develop a mindset that has you and your team fixating on the value of advocacy.

» Visit **www.breakthroughbusinessdevelopment.com** to see updates and insights from the field on this topic and others.

CHAPTER 3
YOUR OVERLOOKED VULNERABILITIES

The goal is to run your business so that it doesn't run you. Paradoxically, this can only happen once you've made yourself obsolete. When the day comes that you don't need to be present and your business can still be productive, you are on the verge of a breakthrough.

David Miller and Duncan MacPherson

Let's get back to the Strategic Analysis. We've talked about some of the untapped opportunities that may exist within your business, which include converting customers to fully empowering clients and then converting them to referral-generating advocates. There is a tremendous array of upside that will come from that and we will outline how you can tap into it.

Now we have to discuss the issues that could be undermining your success and holding you back. This brings us to your potentially overlooked vulnerabilities. In other words, what areas exist within your business that could use some attention? As Andy Grove, one of the founders of Intel, said, "Only the paranoid survive." There is a positive power that can come from negative thinking. Whether or not you feel these issues are relevant to you right now, we want you to consider them because they are crucial for taking your business to the next level. But be proactive about it. You'd never wait for your oil light to come on in your car before you did something about it, would you? The issues we are about to discuss could address why your business is not firing on all cylinders.

THE IMPORTANCE OF ORGANIZATION AND STRUCTURE

The best description we have heard an entrepreneur use to explain his stalled business was simply, "I can't seem to do any more business but I absolutely can't afford to do any less."

Many business professionals find this to be true. Overall, their life is good. They earn a good living and have earned the right to be content. However, deep inside, ambition nags at them. They have hit a plateau but they know there is more upside somewhere. They just can't seem to take their business higher. And, of course, they cannot allow their business to go any lower; after all, they have a lifestyle to support. Fair enough.

So where do they go from here? They could work more hours, but the collateral damage to their personal lives would be unacceptable and would possibly take them down the path of diminishing returns. There is also a fear of rocking the boat. If it isn't really broken, why try to fix it? In other words, if they attempt to tinker with or re-engineer their current approach, they risk adjustments that might not lead to improvements or could possibly even set things back.

As one entrepreneur put it, "I can't afford to be right, *eventually*. My monthly expenses on both a business and personal level require results *right now*." This mindset results in people sticking with the status quo and maintaining a business that simply hovers.

So, you don't want to work any harder. And you're not prepared to resign yourself to "this is as good as it gets." What is the answer? What ingredient is missing?

Just as a piano needs all eighty-eight keys to perform properly, your business needs all of the essential elements to achieve a limitless potential.

MISTAKING MOTION FOR ACTION

When we ask a businessperson, "How are things?" nine times out of ten the answer will be, "I've never been busier." Our response is always, "Busy doing what?" In a lot of cases we see people who are busy but achieving very limited tangible productivity—almost as if they were sewing without a knot at the end of the thread. There is movement and action but little actual traction.

The Law of Cause and Effect reminds us that our activities will determine our productivity. If you want your productivity to increase, the first place you should look is the activities you engage in that give you the best return on your investment of time and energy. Think about it.

The Pareto Principle states that eighty percent of your productivity stems from about twenty percent of your activities. In other words, you make about eighty percent of your income every day in about an hour. So, what goes into that hour? Talking to and meeting with your favorite clients and the most predisposed prospective clients available to you have to be at the top of the list. All other activities must support these two essential activities.

One of the most obvious ways to increase your capacity to do more of what you really get paid to do is to delegate as many supporting activities as possible. Unless you are a one-person operation, this is essential to achieve a breakthrough here. Keep in mind that if you don't have an assistant, you are one yourself. You are doing activities that are preventing you from doing what really matters. And you are being paid accordingly.

For many entrepreneurs, though, managing people and all the accompanying hassles can be a big issue. Many perceive managing more people as potentially amplifying the problem because it can be a distraction. Hiring new people adds yet another expense and could potentially upset the chemistry of the staff currently in place.

These concerns can be addressed if you step back and scrutinize your business. Determine whether it is truly built on predictable, sustainable and duplicable systems driven by accountability and consistency. Does everyone on your team know their job description? Do they follow predetermined systems and procedures, or are they left to their own devices?

We have seen many, many entrepreneurs with successful businesses supported by people who were talented but who unknowingly created self-imposed limitations because, frankly, everyone in the company flew by the seat of their pants. Time after time, the creation of an Organizational Chart followed by the refinement of systems outlined within a Procedures Manual has proven to be essential.

SYSTEMS CREATE SUCCESS

The Organizational Chart is simply a snapshot of everyone on your team with a brief description of what they do—nothing more than a panoramic snapshot of your talent and their tasks. One sheet of paper is required and, when completed, becomes the cover sheet of the Procedures Manual.

Now, if you have never done this before you may be wondering if it is worth the effort. Time and time again, when conducting a Strategic Analysis for one of our coaching and consulting clients, we have determined that in order to develop a systematized business this is an essential step back in order to take several steps forward.

The *Random House Dictionary* defines *systems* as "a group or combination of things or parts forming a complex or unified whole." Does this sound like your business? Dry as it may be, this dictionary definition is critical to your success.

Of particular interest in the definition is the word *unified*. If all the great things you may do in your business are not systemized, or perhaps you have marketing initiatives for some of your clients some of the time but not all of the time, then get serious about installing predictable, sustainable and duplicable systems. Many of our high-caliber coaching and consulting clients, as well as users of the Pareto Platform, got on the right track and realized significant business breakthroughs only after deploying an Organizational Chart for accountability and then, as you will see in a moment, integrating it within a Procedures Manual.

By building what is in essence a "franchise-ready" business, you are making yourself obsolete—and that's a good thing. This is the entrepreneurial paradox—your business does not need you to be present in order for it to be productive. It just chugs along. Take a good, hard look at your operation. Would it continue to function like a Swiss watch if you weren't there all the time? Do you ever answer the phone and have a client ask you if they could speak to your assistant (rather than speak with you) because the client trusts them as much as you? Have you created something with great value, predictable outcomes and ironclad systems? Could you provide documentation detailing exactly how to operate your business right down to the smallest detail? Do you feel that your enterprise is a true business and not just simply a company that sells something?

If you have created a business with true systems, you probably already know the freedom and control it has brought to your business and personal life. The haphazard approach simply cannot compare.

In the spirit of *beginning with the end in mind,* with true systems in place, you are most likely to achieve one of the following:

- the sale of your established business for a substantial profit
- the expansion or franchising of the proprietary approach you've created
- handing your business to the next generation or to a management team so you can take more time off and pursue other interests

None of these scenarios can be realized fully unless, and until, structure and systems are in place and documented.

As an analogy, when driving a car with a standard gearshift in first gear longer than you should, you can almost hear the car breathe a sigh of relief as you shift into second and work your way up to fourth or fifth gear. How can it be that you're accelerating as you're expending less energy? Simply put, everything is just working more efficiently as you gain momentum. Your business should work that way as well. You work diligently and contribute much in the early stages of the business. With time, it should become less draining and start giving back to you.

So where do you start? If you are going to build a business based on systems, the first step is to clearly define each individual's responsibilities within your organization. You and your team have to sit down and determine who does what and when. After all, on a daily basis, you and your team engage in proactive and reactive activities. Based on the Law of Cause and Effect, all of these activities affect your productivity, so you and your team need absolute clarity about who is accountable for each of these activities.

On our website you will find an organizational template that will allow you to create a panoramic snapshot of your business. Think of this as the hub, not only for accountability, but also for consistency.

Remember

» Your goal is to build a business that is productive whether or not you are present and is not at the mercy of maverick talent. You want a business where the tasks and deliverables can be replicated and everyone on your team has account-ability and clarity.

Take Action Now! (Week 1)

» Use the organization and structure template on our website, **www.paretoplatform.com**, to ensure accountability and con-sistency.

» Visit **www.breakthroughbusinessdevelopment.com** to see updates and insights from the field on this topic and others.

CHAPTER 4

THE CREATION AND BENEFITS OF A PROCEDURES MANUAL

Predetermined, documented systems and procedures are steps that add meaningful value to your business and lead to improvements in efficiency and quantifiable breakthroughs in performance.

Duncan MacPherson and David Miller

You and your team undoubtedly execute dozens of routine tasks every day.

There is a good chance that about eighty percent of them are literally performed daily. You have to look at those tasks as proprietary intellectual properties of immense value. Here is the question, though. Where do you store the "schematics" for the inner workings of your company? Are they blueprinted or are they stored in each person's mind? As you will see in a moment, if it's all in your head it's of little value. If it's all in your assistant's or employees' heads it can be downright dangerous.

The Procedures Manual is an extension of the Organizational Chart and is nothing more than a binder containing documentation (descriptions) of the array of tasks and processes you and your team perform. In concert with the Organizational Chart, this tool becomes a process map where every action your team performs is clearly described, from the very mundane tasks, such as the maintaining of the various office supplies you want on hand at any given time, as well as where you buy them and where you store them, to more sophisticated tasks, such as your process for meeting with a prospective client for the first time, determining a fit and fast-tracking new clients to advocate status. We don't mean to oversimplify, but it's not as complicated as it sounds.

More often than not, when we raise this topic with one of our consulting clients, the immediate response is either "this sounds like work" or "I can't really see the payoff here."

It *is* work. But you can have eighty percent of this done in the next two weeks. It *can* be done. We know. If you use the templates from our website and tell all your staff that over the next two weeks you want everyone to document their daily tasks, it *will* get done.

And remember, *done* matters more than *perfect*. (This stems from the countless times an entrepreneur-client of ours has called in a panic to tell us that a key support person just gave two weeks' notice. Sure enough, the Manual was completed before the departure and the new person took it and ran with it immediately.)

And this leads to the payoff issue. Your company won't have a dependency problem—meaning it won't be dependent on any given staff member, including yourself. Every task is documented and can be replicated by virtually anyone.

It is remarkably revealing when we ask entrepreneurs what would happen if they took a month off, starting tomorrow. We have received a great many downright shocking and funny responses over the years. The most illuminating was "The only thing scarier than that is the thought of what would happen if my assistant took a month off tomorrow. And I don't even really know what she does, but my clients love her."

It's one thing to say you have to be present for your business to be productive. But it's another thing altogether to say that you are at the mercy of maverick talent. How much of a setback would it be if one of your key staff members left in two weeks? We've seen the departure of one key person put a business owner into a six-month rut and in some cases a tailspin. Can you imagine how powerful it would be if you hired a replacement, plugged the new person into your Organizational Chart and then handed him or her your Procedures Manual and said, "Here is how we do things around here—just add water!"?

More important, by creating what is essentially a franchise-ready business—a business with duplicable procedures—the value of your business will increase. If you were to sell your business, you could show your Procedures Manual to the suitor during the due diligence process and explain how he or she could easily replicate your success.

The manual ensures you are running the business instead of it running you. You could take more time off without worrying that it's all unraveling without you. You could expand with certainty and efficiency. Your team would have focus and accountability rather than being left to their own devices. Even if none of those benefits appeal to you, we'll say it again: You've given a lot to your business and it's time for the business to give a little back. This is the first step in that direction.

And finally, and most importantly, this approach is the bedrock for creating quite simply the most important ingredient for meaningful relationships with loyal advocates—trust. People stay loyal to people they trust. People empower people they trust and people refer friends to people they trust. Here's a question: Who is it easier for you to trust and refer a close friend to—a salesperson or a consultant? Salespeople master a pitch and try to close sales. Consultants master procedures and strive for lasting relationships built on trust.

THE FOUR Cs OF ADVOCACY

Trust is created by what we call the four Cs: credentials, consistency, congruency and chemistry. *Credentials* means you have the goods to deliver solutions that at least meet, or ideally exceed, client expectations. *Consistency* means you do things the same way, time after time. *Congruency* means you do what you say, and *chemistry* means you know your clients inside out. A Procedures Manual goes such a long way to helping you and your team bring the four Cs to life habitually and create an experience that is meaningful and memorable for clients.

Habits and procedures are crucial to success. Look at top caliber pilots. Even though they could fly a plane in their sleep, they still follow their flight manuals and rely on habits and rituals to consistently re-create a successful flight. This adherence to procedure enables them to respond confidently when the unexpected arises. Perhaps you heard or read about the stories of Coast Guard helicopter pilots that arrived on the scene to help out victims of the Katrina hurricane disaster. One pilot from Alaska would jump into a helicopter with another pilot from Maine and even though they had never flown together they were up in the air as if they could read each others' thoughts. They had been trained the same way using the same Procedures Manual and as a result they were predictably efficient and productive.

We can learn something from how journalists work. Journalists use a procedure called W5—what, when, where, why and who—to diagnose a situation and create compelling, informative articles.

This format is virtually subconscious because of its repetition; it actually liberates the journalists to be more nimble and creative. Good actors use scripts, yet seem spontaneous and unrehearsed. Most of your life is a collection of habits and rituals. The way you shower, the way you drive to work, even the way you mow the lawn, is often a pattern you've repeated. As such, the results are consistent. Your business should be no different except for the fact that it must be documented.

At this point, if we have drifted into completely foreign territory and you're wondering if there is an example of how this has actually benefited an entrepreneur, allow us to give you this one. Do you know of Ray Kroc's story? Ray Kroc sold milkshake makers and straws to restaurants in America. One day he walked into the original McDonald's Brothers' restaurant, back when they only had one arch! Way ahead of his time, Ray Kroc secured the international franchise rights for that restaurant. The first thing he did was document everything in a binder. You know what they've done since then? They've sold that binder around the world more than thirty thousand times. They put the pickles on the hamburgers in the exact same way in every restaurant in every city in every country around the world. There are no maverick hamburger-makers left to their own devices being creative with the ketchup gun. This is just one of countless examples of entrepreneurs who propelled their businesses to completely new levels through the deployment of a Procedures Manual.

Let's say you really get ambitious and decide to expand your business. How powerful would it be if all new staff members were shown exactly how to do their jobs and be empowered by such clarity? That is pure scalability. They wouldn't have to reinvent the wheel or try to figure things out for themselves. It would no longer be a mentor-protégé relationship; it would be about authentic and predictable leverage. Accountability (ensuring staff members add to profits, not costs) and consistency (ensuring no deviations) would become a certainty.

Again, we realize this task can seem daunting and there is often an urge to rule this idea out either because of the hassle factor or because of the perception that the benefits don't measure up to the investment of time to get it done. One client comes to mind. He had the "why bother" attitude until we asked him to reflect on how he addressed issues of poor consistency within his company. When a breakdown occurred in the past with a team member, the entrepreneur would call a meeting and give everyone a speech about the merits of service. Everyone nodded in agreement and he sent them all back to work freshly motivated. He felt good about himself after the speech, too. Unfortunately, the benefits of his speech lasted about three days and then things went off track again. To make matters worse, often he would simply do things himself rather than teach his people to do them, rationalizing in his mind that it would take him less time to do it than to explain it. You can see how this can become a slippery slope to self-imposed limitations within a business. This same entrepreneur, after finally creating an Organizational Chart and Procedures Manual, now takes more time off than ever before and is enjoying levels of success and predictability that he only dreamed about in the past.

If you "get it," so to speak, and are in fact eager to get started, please don't fall into the paralysis trap, trying to make this concept perfect. Yes, constant refinement and the pursuit of excellence are encouraged, but your business will never be perfect. Think of artists who realize that works of art are never really finished, but rather abandoned! They could keep rewriting and tweaking the lyrics of songs or adding more detail to paintings, but at some point they have to walk away resigned to the fact that they are done and need to move on to the next project.

Remember

> » Your Procedures Manual can be eighty percent done in two weeks and is essential to creating liberation and order in your business and your life.

Take Action Now! (Weeks 2 & 3)

> » Use the Procedures Manual template on our website, **www. paretoplatform.com**, to create your Procedures Manual.

> » Visit **www.breakthroughbusinessdevelopment.com** to see updates and insights from the field on this topic and others.

CHAPTER 5
CLIENT CLASSIFICATION AND TRIPLE-A—AN IDEAL CLIENT PROFILE

Growth is for vanity—profit and progress are for sanity.

Entrepreneurial Truism

A re you focused on growth or on progress? Growth means bigger; profit and progress means better. The entrepreneurial fallacy is *grow or perish*. Many business people have a "growth at all costs" mindset, but for many, unbridled growth can hurt more than it helps over the long haul. Of course, for some companies—large ones especially—well-managed, continual growth is an essential and effective strategy. (Toyota and GE seem to have it figured out, whereas Ford and Airbus seem to have misfired here and there.)

We often reveal to entrepreneurs that perhaps their goal shouldn't be to see how big they can get but rather how small they can stay. You can imagine that for some people this seems completely counterintuitive. After all, more is more. (Some people get so confused by this that they look at us the same way a dog looks when you hold him up to a mirror.)

Don't get us wrong—we want your productivity and profitability to grow, but that doesn't mean the number of client relationships you manage also has to grow. (As you will see in a moment, the first can increase while the second declines.) Do you know your capacity? By that we mean, how many client relationships can your current infrastructure support before opportunity leakage and collateral damage creep in?

One of the first times this really occurred to us was when a business owner, referred to us by a client, said a few things that turned the proverbial lightbulb on for us. Fifteen minutes into the conversation, we learned he was making a ton of money, had close to nine hundred clients, was building this colossal business and had no life. He was stressed out, in poor shape, and had stuff going on at home that we couldn't believe he'd tell us. (You may have heard the saying, "You are only as happy as your least happy child." Well, this guy had some serious collateral damage building in his life as a result of his obsession with business.) And yet he said to us, "I've heard good things about you guys. I'm thinking about hiring you to help me *grow* my business."

Our first reaction was to say, "We don't know each other very well but probably based on what you've told us, the best thing we can help you do is dismantle this thing." Well, didn't he go ballistic! He was shocked, then defensive, and then downright angry. "What are you talking about? My business is booming! I'm a member of our national Chairman's Council. I'm a poster boy in our industry!" (Translation: Do you have any idea how important I think I am?)

So we explained, "Listen, this track you're on is costing you more than it's getting you. You're all over the map and because of your approach you are on a collision course with some serious issues down the road. It's just our opinion. But with all due respect, you sound stressed." You know what he was doing to relieve stress? He had gone to Costco and bought a $59 water fountain that gurgled water in his office all day to create a relaxing atmosphere, and he listened to Enya CDs in his car on the way to and from work.

He finally relented when we asked, "Do you have an Ideal Client Profile? Who is your ideal client? Describe your ideal client. You are building your business a mile wide and an inch deep." He was like the hunter who walked into the forest and randomly fired his rifle and said, "Let's see if something runs into that." We told him he needed to be far more methodical and precise in terms of how he built his business and what kind of clients he was striving to attract.

GETTING STARTED

Think of your ideal client. What makes him or her meet that criteria? You like them, they value your services, they don't pester you to lower fees, they refer people to you. Remember, we didn't say "best client"; we said "ideal," as in favorite client. Most entrepreneurs describe an ideal client with a singular issue in mind—how much revenue he or she generates for their business. It goes much deeper than that.

We ask our clients to take a panoramic view when describing their ideal clients and we urge them to apply our Triple-A process. **The first A of the Ideal Client Profile is simple—** ***action.*** To what degree does the ideal client have to take action with you to be considered the perfect relationship? How much revenue does the action typically have to generate? Keep in mind, when you think about the ideal client we want you to think of the word *fit.* Your expertise and the solutions you provide are a perfect fit for whom? Define that person. They have needs and you have skills to match those needs—describe those needs. As you will see, this becomes a tool that is very attractive to high-caliber clients in keeping with projecting a specialist approach. By that we mean that high-caliber clients want to know that your skills are coveted by people like themselves and there is cachet in dealing with you based on your expertise.

The second A is *attitude*. The ideal client has a great attitude, sees your value and empowers you as their sole provider. Even if a client is top of the action list, a lousy attitude can hurt more than help your business. As an example, the ideal client doesn't focus on what you cost; he focuses on what you're worth to him—your dependability and value. The ideal client doesn't feel you are a commodity to the point where he is constantly questioning or maligning your fees or pricing. The ideal client doesn't also deal with your competitors, making him only a customer.

The third A is *advocacy*. The ideal client is actually an advocate—fiercely loyal, fully empowering, a joy to work with, loved by your team, and ready to brag about you to anybody who'll listen. Advocates appreciate the merits of *buying into* a relationship with a professional rather than simply *buying something* from a vendor.

Take a look at your client base and determine who meets your ideal client profile, or at least has the ability to in the near future. These are your Triple-A clients. Strive to clone and competitor-proof them. They are an asset that needs to be guarded. Most of all, they deserve your attention. A great many people out there need you, but it is an error in judgment to spend time with people who need you at the expense of people who deserve you.

And remember the Law of Environment, which tells us that your favorite clients will live near, work with and refer people pretty much like themselves. Sure, there are exceptions to every rule, but put the odds in your favor and consider this law carefully, and not solely from an income perspective.

There is a personal development issue here—we are products of our environment. (As an example, spend a month in Milwaukee, Toronto or Liverpool—it doesn't take long to subconsciously take on some of the local accent.) With that in mind, don't just ask what you're earning from your business, also think about who you're becoming over the years. Few things impact who we're becoming more than the people we're around on an ongoing basis. And to that end, some relationships are far more worth it than others. Remember, it's not the snake bite that kills you, it's the venom that slowly but surely works its way through your system. It takes time but it will take you down. Toxic relationships can wear you down over time, too.

It is for that reason that you absolutely must have rules of engagement in place that guide you in terms of who you will accept as a client. If you are in a transactional business, like the injury lawyer we mentioned earlier, this isn't all that relevant, but it is crucial if you are in the business of building long-term relationships. By rules of engagement we really mean that how you start a relationship and the parameters you use for selecting who you will work with will have a profound impact on how the relationship will unfold over time.

Keep in mind that while actions can change, attitudes rarely do. A classic example is when you meet with a prospective client for the first time and they start grinding you on the price of your fees or solutions. How do you respond when a fee vigilante walks into your office and says, "I met with one of your competitors and they agreed to lower their fees."? Do you get defensive and start selling harder? That would be chasing. Do you cave in and meet the discount, or do you step back and say something that is so thought-provoking that it stops the prospective client in his tracks and favorably contrasts your value with a competitor's? That is the essence of attracting. Can you do this in a way that enables the prospective client to conclude that you are the superior option?

Here is an example of what our clients say when this scenario presents itself:

> **Prospective client:** Will you lower your fees to match a competitor?
>
> **You:** I hear where you're coming from. We all want to be intelligent with how we spend money. However, you need to know something, I NEVER NEGOTIATE MY VALUE! You see, if a competitor is prepared to lower his or her price, they are just trying to make a sale. They are asking you to buy something and they are focusing on the commissions they will earn. I ask my clients to buy into a lasting relationship. I focus on the lifetime value of my relationships. If this is what is important to you, I think you are going to overlook what is utterly important over the lifetime of this relationship, and for that reason I am probably not the provider for you, because I never negotiate my value.

If only we had a buck for every time a client of ours used a variation of that approach to convey the rules of engagement, and either on the spot or even a week later the prospective client said to our client, "Okay, I get it. You're right. Everyone else is just trying to make a sale. I know where you stand. Will you accept me as a client?"

We're not suggesting this will happen every time, but think about this: Do you really want a client who fixates on what you cost when his or her attitude will likely never change over time? It requires very little skill to start a relationship based on a price reduction. Again, if you have a transactional business, well, you live by the rules you set. But if you are focusing on advocacy, you have to stay true to yourself. It's like when Picasso was asked in Paris to sketch a portrait of a woman. In just a few minutes he finished his work and handed it to her and insisted on a fee of several thousand dollars. Shocked, she said, "Several thousand dollars for something you created in mere minutes?" Picasso replied, "It took me all my life to do that!" That is the essence of understanding one's own value.

Once you've identified your existing and Triple-A clients, you then need to assign a classification for your remaining clients so that you can begin to delineate the level of service you provide going forward. (This is not about being disrespectful or elitist, it's about putting yourself on a track to consistently and predictably attract the type of client you want.) Examples would be Double-A clients—those who take action and have good attitudes yet never send referrals (these are potential Triple-As with a little coaching). A Single-A client would be someone who takes action but has a poor attitude and isn't an advocate. You could then create B, C and D client lists to describe the degree of action these customers take.

As you will see later on, this classification tool will be directly linked to your Client Service Matrix. This matrix will outline the degree of service each client receives. This is essential because virtually every business reflects the Pareto Principle—again, that eighty percent of their business is generated by about twenty percent of their clients. The Client Service Matrix ensures that the most deserving twenty percent of your clients receive eighty percent of your time and attention.

THE UPSIDE TO RIGHTSIZING

After you have established your Ideal Client Profile, you have an important and perhaps difficult decision to make about current clients who don't meet your profile. Do you keep them as clients, or not? Can they become advocates? Do lower-value clients have an adverse impact on your capacity to serve newly attracted Triple-A clients? Do these people have too high a hassle effect on you and your team to be worth the effort?

We understand that some of these people have been with you since day one and may be like family to you, but chances are that there are some clients that you should disassociate from. You may be reluctant to part with the income they bring and you can make exceptions, but be practical and realistic and try to step beyond emotion and sentiment.

Some business owners hear the concept of rightsizing and misinterpret it as an opportunity to fire some clients. They begrudgingly did business with these people over the years and felt liberated when we told them they should take action and part company. They envisioned an opportunity to "give them a piece of their mind" and kick them out.

That's not what we're talking about here. The last thing any industry needs is businesspeople firing clients. If you have too many clients or if they do not meet your profile, you are doing them—and yourself—a disservice by keeping them. Be professional and gracefully bow out of relationships where the chemistry is poor between you and your client or where the hassle factor is high. Take the high road no matter how much friction or resentment has built up.

RESPECTFUL DISASSOCIATION

When you have identified clients who aren't a good fit for you going forward, call each of them with a forthright and rational approach, such as the following.

> Until recently, I've been trying to be all things to all people. Over time, I found myself becoming a generalist. I feel that as a result, things are starting to fall through the cracks. Going forward, I've decided to become a specialist who strives to be all things to some people. I know my capacity, and in

order to offer superior service, I have to make some changes to my business. Part of that includes using an Ideal Client Profile that reflects the type of client who is a good fit for my team and me.

At this point, elaborate upon your Triple-A criteria.

Based on this profile and our history together, I feel there isn't a good fit between us going forward. However, as a service to you I have identified someone else I feel would be a better fit for you and I will make the introduction, if you would like.

You will—frankly—be amazed at the outcome of this exchange. Either the client will agree and move on effortlessly or they will fight to stay on board with you. They'll say such things as "It never occurred to me that I should empower you fully." Or, "I can move everything to you." Or, "I'm sorry if I've been rude to your staff—it wasn't intentional." You may even hear "I didn't know you were accepting new clients, but I can easily start referring people to you."

You can decide to keep the client on board, conditionally, if they agree to respect the rules of engagement, those rules being that they strive to become a Triple-A client.

You didn't start your business with these rules—you have developed them as you evolved and are only now telling your clients your expectations. Given the opportunity and a clear understanding of your new mandate, many of these people will gratefully evolve from being simply customers into being true advocates. They do so because you clearly explain why it matters and how they will benefit. In some instances your instincts will tell you the client is not really going to respond favorably over time. Maintain your integrity. Some will try to convince you they can change, but when you sense they are simply paying lip service or if your instincts tell you to steer clear, be professional but firm. Remember, actions can change, yet attitudes rarely do.

> **You:** I just don't think there is a good fit going forward.
>
> **Client:** I can change. I didn't mean to be a pain to your people.
>
> **You:** I just don't think there is a good fit, but I'll introduce you to...
>
> **Client:** But I don't want to work with anyone else.
>
> **You:** I appreciate that, but based on the direction I'm taking, I just don't think there is a good fit here.

You may have to be like a broken record repeating your position. In the back of your mind, consider that the point of rightsizing is to build a clientele composed exclusively of people with whom you want to work with. These are the clients who will turn into flag wavers and sing your praises to their friends, family and associates. These clients are the key to building a successful, profitable business, which gives you time to enjoy the things that matter to you.

Remember

» The clients who generate eighty percent of your revenue deserve eighty percent of your time. This group rarely exceeds twenty percent of your clientele.

Take Action Now! (Week 2)

» Create a Triple-A Ideal Client Profile using the template found on our website, **www.paretoplatform.com**, and stick to it ardently.

» Visit **www.breakthroughbusinessdevelopment.com** to see updates and insights from the field on this topic and others.

CHAPTER 6
BUILD CLIENT CHEMISTRY WITH FORM

Chemistry with your clients is just as important as
your credentials and competencies as a business
professional.

Duncan MacPherson and David Miller

When we work with an entrepreneur on an individual consulting basis, we strive to help him or her create a code of conduct that creates long-term client relationships built on trust. As we mentioned, the four Cs of advocacy that create trust are credentials, consistency, congruency and chemistry. We'll assume that you have made the commitment to be leading edge in your sector in terms of credentials and that you can "deliver the goods," so to speak. By creating an Organizational Chart integrated with a Procedures Manual, you will achieve consistency. By maintaining a forthright consultative approach, you will create congruency. But focusing solely on those three is not always enough. Creating chemistry with clients goes a long way towards insulating you from external issues and making you less vulnerable. So, how do you create chemistry?

Think about your client conversations. Clients reveal things to you that go beyond what they are buying from you. Do you view that information as invaluable and proprietary intellectual property? Do you capture and chronicle that information? The following is a proven process that enables you to invest every conversation with a client into the rest of the relationship and in the process build chemistry by showing each of your Triple-A clients that you are interested in them. It may sound trite, but it's just as important that you be interested as it is to be interesting. That interest in your clients builds chemistry and chemistry builds trust.

An easy way to achieve that is to create *FORM* profiles for each of your Triple-A clients. FORM is an acronym that represents the four key components to a typical client relationship. Strive to learn and document as much as you can in all four areas. This information is proprietary and invaluable.

The F in FORM stands for *family*. Learn everything you possibly can about the families of your Triple-A clients and capture this information in a profile that you and your team can refer to, and then look for ways to bring value to this area in the future. The following is an example of the power of understanding a client's family and paying attention to their concerns. One of our favorite consulting clients came to us in a very somber mood, so we asked, "What's up?" He proceeded to tell us that something dreadful had happened to a client's family member. This client had come to him and bared his soul. "He told you that?" we couldn't help but ask. "That says a lot about your relationship. It's a moment of truth and certainly defines your relationship. What are you going to do?" Our client said he didn't know. "You *have* to respond to this," we advised him. "Buy the book, *When Bad Things Happen to Good People*, and send it to your client with a card saying something like 'I'm thinking about you. I know it's a tough time, but please call me if you just need to chat.'" His client called a few days later to say that it was the most thoughtful thing anybody had done during that difficult time.

Not all opportunities to pay attention will be that dramatic. The point is that it is important to encourage your clients to talk to you about their families and to capture that information and respond accordingly. We're not suggesting that you get in to the gift-giving business. We are recommending you look for ways to show your clients that you're paying attention.

O stands for *occupation*. Know what your Triple-A clients do. Learn to understand their business. Be aware of their trials, tribulations and triumphs and look for ways to bring value to them in this area. Again, when a circumstance arises that merits your attention, respond in a meaningful manner. We know of accountants and financial advisors who have made themselves indispensable to their business-owner clients by becoming sounding boards and confidants with respect to business issues. Could you imagine the impact of giving a business-owner client some tips on how to attract referrals or how to run their business more effectively? We've seen the benefits in terms of increased loyalty and refer-ability.

R is for *recreation*. All of us enjoy both goal-achieving and tension-relieving activities. When your clients talk about their hobbies and recreational interests, listen carefully. Do your clients like wine, golf, tennis and/or travel? Make notes and look for ways to bring value in these areas. Over time you'll notice interesting commonalities among your best clients and their recreational interests. That information can be very valuable when it comes to a client appreciation event, gifts, and so forth.

Finally, the M stands for your *message*. The products and services you sell and the solutions or expertise you provide are your message. You are the messenger. When a prospective client meets you for the first time, are they connecting with your message or are they connecting with you, the messenger? When your best client waves your flag to their friend, what does that client spend more time bragging about, the message or the messenger? When a client leaves you and goes to a competitor, why do they leave? Is it due to dissatisfaction with the message or because of some kind of disconnect between them and the messenger?

We will never trivialize what you deliver, in terms of your services and solutions, but realize that your message is probably not truly proprietary. There are others who can do what you do. And bringing good value in terms of your message is what your clients expect. Your goal is to exceed their expectations. Delivering your message with quality is essential, but paying attention to the other areas of the client's life is what will help you stand out from the pack and be memorable in the minds of your clients. Clearly, if you are in a one-off transactional business this isn't an essential concept. But if you want to competitor-proof your clients, gain their full empowerment and improve your refer-ability over the long haul, it comes down to trust. Building chemistry goes a long way to achieving that.

It's one thing to know your Triple-A client inside out; it's quite another thing to create a system and process to ensure that information is really serving you well. By this point in your relationships with your current Triple-A clients, you already know a great deal about them. If you're like most entrepreneurs we know, you keep this incredibly valuable information in your head. Let's just back up a few steps—is that a *predictable, sustainable and duplicable system?* If this information about your most valuable asset—your Triple-A clients—is in your head, it's definitely not intellectual property and is not a fully maximized asset. And it is most definitely not something your team can use if you're not present.

Some entrepreneurs trivialize this concept and feel that simply delivering a good product or service is enough. Again, your solutions and services are not enough to be considered a Unique Value Proposition (UVP). And we'll say this again, too—it is a given that you deliver good solutions, but your competitors are continually trying to best you in that regard, thus making your solutions more commoditized each and every day. The one thing your competitors cannot do with as much success as you is develop chemistry with *your* clients. Your clients do not and will not reveal nearly as much information to a competitor courting them as they will to a trusted provider such as you are, or can be.

Our best advice to any entrepreneur whose business has hit a plateau and who is looking to take it to the next level is simply this: Get to know everything you can about your best clients and chronicle that information within a system. Whether you use our Pareto Platform or some other CRM or even just simple file folders, you must have an integrated mechanism that transforms everything a client reveals to you into invaluable, actionable, intellectual property.

Think about it. In a typical twenty-minute conversation with a great client, you talk about his family and his business, perhaps his hobbies, as well as the solutions and services you provide, your message.

The family, occupation and recreation information can be incredibly valuable. Relationships become stronger every time a client reveals something not related to business. These are *moments of truth.* And when a client reveals something personal, he is essentially saying, "I trust you."

Here's an example to help get your wheels turning. One of your best clients informs you he and his wife just had a baby. Do you enter the event into your client profile and send a small thoughtful gift, like a soothing CD of Mozart for Kids and a card to congratulate them?

Again, we're not suggesting you get into the gift-giving business. It's more important to be thoughtful than it is to spend a lot of money. But sometimes a meaningful moment of truth with a client justifies a response of some kind.

If you send a small gift to pay tribute to a milestone such as a birthday, anniversary or meaningful achievement, ensure what you send has both impact and shelf life. *Impact* means something personalized that speaks to them. The information you captured with FORM can guide you in that regard. This initiative is value-added, but it's only valuable if it's something the client actually values. *Shelf life* simply means that what you send will stick around for a while.

Moments of truth will be numerous, varied and ongoing. As your relationships with your clients unfold, grow and develop, you will undoubtedly find a great deal of satisfaction, to say nothing of increased advocacy, from responding to those moments with consideration, respect and a bit of imagination.

As another example, a client tells you he'll be embarking on a substantial vacation with his family. Why not send a gift basket to the hotel as a welcome upon their arrival?

Perhaps you taste a terrific new wine at the local wine festival. You think of a great client with whom you've just celebrated a ten-year business anniversary, and who also appreciates fine wine. Why not pay tribute with a thank you card, a nice corkscrew and a bottle of this new wine?

Whatever your view is on this concept, consider what Bernard Malamud said: "As you value the lives of others, yours achieves value."

THESE FUNDAMENTAL STRATEGIES MAKE THIS APPROACH EFFECTIVE

1. Be targeted. We're not suggesting you do this with every client and every moment of truth. At the very least, start with your

best and favorite Triple-A clients. They are the most deserving. They bring the most value to your business. They take action on a consistent basis, have a great attitude, and are predisposed to advocacy.

2. Make it a habit. The FORM process must become habitual and part of your day-to-day code of conduct. Empower your team to view this as an essential activity and to take the necessary actions.

3. Be unique. Develop your own recognizable style by doing something out of the ordinary, something memorable. Whether you deliver pumpkins to your clients before Halloween or send Thanksgiving cards, strive to stand out from the pack.

4. Be consistent. Trust is broken when your client's expectations of you are not met. If you are all over the map, randomly dabbling at things, you'll be conspicuous by your lack of consistency.

GET ON IT!

Many businesspeople hear about the FORM concept and say to themselves, "This is a good idea. I should do this." A week later, nothing has happened. The Law of Diminishing Intent kicked in and the status quo prevailed. The best are separated from the rest in business because the best understand that a good idea not implemented is worthless. We'll discuss this in more detail in the Reality Check section. In the meantime, keep in mind that the best set out to make good ideas habitual by creating a process. They strike while the proverbial iron is hot and quickly translate a good idea into results. They also empower their teams to use their judgment to execute the process.

Consider the following information and strive to document as much as you can for all Triple-A clients in these categories:

Family

- the usual suspects: names, ages, birthdays of all immediate family members (send cards)
- children's school placement, semester, fast-tracking, university program (send graduation gifts)
- children's milestones: first jobs, driver's license (send recognition gifts to child)
- children's activities: sports, competitions, dance, music (send recognition to child)
- children's holiday plans: travel, camps (send information articles)
- family pet(s): type, name, age, breed, specific problems, kenneling, kenneling rates (send informative articles)

In paying attention to the next generation, you are, as Confucius said, "Digging your well before you're thirsty." This is especially crucial if you do business with second-generation clients. If you've read *The Millionaire Next Door*, you know all about the issues that can arise. It reminds us of what is often referred to as The Levis Syndrome. Back in the day, Levis owned the jeans market. But things started to slide over time, primarily because the next generation wasn't buying Levis jeans. Why not, you ask? Because apparently it's not cool to wear the same kind of jeans your parents wear!

Occupation

- job promotion (send congratulatory gift)
- job loss or business setback (send "You'll land on your feet!" card)

- community service recognition (send congratulatory gift)
- moonlighting activities (send information articles if client is exploring a possible future line of work)
- volunteer activities (consider partnering or fundraising with client's chosen organization)
- duplicate all of the above for spousal inquiries

Recreation

- type of holiday property owned and location (send fix-up articles)
- if holiday property is paid off (discuss asset management)
- whether holiday property is used as rental income source (send tax articles)
- recreational activities engaged in (send subscription to specialty magazines)
- travel holidays planned (send interest articles)
- leisure activities of client (send special event invitations)
- health-related issues: broach health topics only when a client raises the issue in response to a "How are things in general?" question; e.g., if you learn a client has quit smoking, send a congratulatory card/gift with words of encouragement
- duplicate all of the above for spousal inquiries

Message

- Anything and everything that relates to the products and services you provide!

Remember

» This is the best FORMula for building chemistry and is a crucial component for delivering the four Cs.

Take Action Now! (Week 4)

» Use the FORM Client Profiling Tool found on our website, **www.paretoplatform.com**, and begin to deploy it with your Triple-A clients.

» Visit **www.breakthroughbusinessdevelopment.com** to see updates and insights from the field on this topic and others.

PART 2:
TARGETS AND GOALS
(WEEK 4)

CHAPTER 7

SUCCESS IS ACHIEVED BY DESIGN, NOT BY CHANCE

Invest your past into the future.

Jim Rohn

The Strategic Analysis step in our STAR approach is essentially designed to help you look closely at and make critical observations about your business. The Targets and Goals step is designed to help you look forward. We get excited talking about this concept because this exact process has not only been helpful for a variety of our clients, but it's also helped us to achieve meaningful goals ourselves.

We can face the future in one of two ways: with anticipation or with apprehension. How do we face the future with *anticipation*? We design it.

Having goals enables us to see past obstacles and prevents us from drifting off track. We all have a tendency to drift. It's natural because of the distractions, external issues and interruptions that occur on a daily basis. We get faked out and sometimes become lulled into ignoring the track we should be running on.

Clearly set goals rejuvenate us and restore our enthusiasm. Additionally, by setting goals, we're reminded that we must be nimble and adaptable and the game plan we rely on must be flexible to account for Murphy's Law. Where you want to go won't necessarily change, but how you get there, after a few hurdles present themselves, may change. Our goals pull us back on track.

Getting and staying on track is a critical benefit of the goal-setting process, and we say this based on personal experiences. We know firsthand that your trajectory determines your destination. Jim Rohn, legendary personal development guru, said that "the winds of opportunity blow the same for everybody. The difference is in how you set your sails to harness the wind." Your plan and your goals are your sails.

Furthermore, today there often seems to be such a fixation on the negative, and this can take us off our path. Everywhere we turn, we are being told about all the bad things that are happening locally and internationally. As a result, a lot of people develop reactive thoughts and get bogged down in focusing on events, circumstances and surroundings that aren't at all positive. This creates a mindset where these people focus on what they don't want in life rather than on what they do want.

We come back full circle to the Law of Attraction. We believe, as cosmic as this may sound, that thoughts are things. By that we mean that what we think and visualize plays a huge role in our reality. This goes beyond affirmation and a positive attitude. Think of it this way. If you play golf and you aren't playing particularly well on a given day, it might help to try pumping yourself up with positive self-talk. You could say to yourself, "I'm better than this. I'm a good golfer." That's certainly better than saying to yourself, "Stop swinging so hard, you dummy!"

It's always better to focus on what you propose than on what you oppose, but at the same time you must recognize and affirm the reality of the situation. Otherwise you're on the verge of being delusional. However, what if you were to actually visualize yourself swinging smoothly with perfect tempo? Is it possible that your body could recreate that vision? Professional athletes would tell you that they often see themselves performing the way they want to before they actually do it. It's true that what you internalize will often be actualized. As Wayne Dyer would say, "You'll believe it when you see it." Setting targets and goals will help you see what you want before you achieve it.

Now, some people hear this and halfheartedly apply it, but quickly get discouraged because the results aren't always instantaneous. Remind yourself that true success is incremental. It takes time. It builds slowly. Having goals enables us to build the bridge as we cross it, because we know what's on the other side. We can go ahead with confidence and courage because we know where we're going. Just as you can drive quickly down a highway at night even though all you can actually see is the short distance in front of you illuminated by your headlights, your goals give you a vision of what's out there for you.

GOALS ARE THE WHY; STRATEGY IS THE HOW

As business consultants, we are constantly asked *how* to do this, that and the other thing. Clients want to know how to competitor-proof their clients, how to attract more referrals, how to generate more revenue, and so on. As we've alluded to, the "how" is the process, but the "why" speaks to purpose, and purpose is just as important as process. The goals you set are a major component of your sense of purpose and personal motivation, which is why we put such a big emphasis on the topic.

Before we actually walk you through our goal-setting approach, it's a good idea to crystallize your values and philosophy on paper. What do you stand for and what parameters will you stay within as you embark on your journey? This is not a mission statement, but rather a reminder to yourself about your core values and personal integrity. We have done this ourselves and we came up with this simple statement:

> We are in business to deliver value to our clients, our staff and ourselves. We will never strive to make a profit at the expense of anyone but rather will make a profit through the service of others. In our enlightened self-interest, we will also strive to never do things at our own expense. We know that the best way to take care of those around us is to take impeccable care of ourselves. Self-sacrifice breeds contempt, while self-interest breeds respect. We will strive to leave a profit in our community by leaving things better than we found them. Our conduct today is reflected on our legacy tomorrow and we will never sell out on what we stand for.

That might sound a little lofty or idealistic, but we do take pride in trying to ensure that we live up to it. It's part of our purpose. Some people talk about a calling. Well, we feel that your purpose is what you say it is. It's self-defined. And it provides fertile soil for passion and the belief that what you do matters and is making a difference.

We mention this now because as you go through our goal-setting exercise, we want you to consider the full spectrum of what you want to achieve. As you can imagine, if we asked ten businesspeople to tell us their goals, nine of the ten will focus on only one aspect: money. Don't misunderstand us—we want you to earn as much as you possibly can, but we also want you to remember that money doesn't make us valuable. The goal is not just to see how much we earn. The goal is to see who we become. We all know this to be important and true. Think about it. Have you heard the old expression that "every life is either a warning or an example"? We've all met some rich warnings. We've all met some rich jerks. The world is full of teachers we can learn from.

So, consider all aspects of your life. Financial goals are important but alone can often be anticlimactic (kind of like when a friend gives a bottle of wine for your birthday and then announces he made it himself). Most people are motivated by the things that come with having money: free time, travel, fine dining, a new house or the benefits for family and community. Don't hesitate to include any and all goals and objectives from all facets of your life. They ensure that you don't strive to make money at the expense of other things that are more important.

SOMETHING TO THINK ABOUT

> It's hard to make predictions, especially about the future.
>
> Yogi Berra
>
> (*No book like this would be complete without a quote from Yogi.*)

Consider the following exercise. You can print them from our website and spend some time writing your answers.

1. List three things you accomplished last year that you are especially proud of.

All of us have achieved something meaningful. Stop for a moment and savor that. The pace of business today doesn't allow us much time to sit back and reflect. Perhaps you overcame some adversity or achieved a meaningful milestone through your resilience.

You've heard the old maxim: Circumstances don't make the man, they reveal him. Adversity is a far better coach than success. We all love hearing stories of entrepreneurs who overcome adversity. As business consultants, we've often seen that it was a moment of adversity that revealed true greatness in a client, while prosperity concealed it. None of us can deny, however, that talking about adversity is much easier (and far more interesting to others) after we've overcome it. Adversity can serve us when we account for it and reflect on our accomplishments.

Whatever you've accomplished in the last year, and we're sure there are some great things, take a few moments to remind yourself. It's a big deal and here's why. A common trap that many people, including us, fall into is one where they set a goal for the future that they become obsessed with and then emotionally disappear until they achieve it. You can't focus on the future if it means you will be vacant in the present. That is a recipe for regret. The essence of Zen is that you could live to be one hundred or it could all be over tomorrow. A balance between hoping for tomorrow with a positive experience for today is essential. We all should spend more time appreciating what we have even as we aspire to what we don't have. It will also help if you talk and think in the present tense. By that we mean, rather than saying you're going to get into better shape, you could say you *are* getting in better shape.

2. **Write seven things on your five-year wish list.**

Do you want to sell your business? Do you want to take more time off? We have some clients who take four months off a year. (We're not sure if you're into that kind of thing, but it certainly works for them!) Perhaps you want to expand your business. Maybe you want to run a marathon. Write it all down. And don't stop at seven things. Write as much as you like. Where do you want to go? What do you want to do? What do you want to achieve? What do you want to become? How much money do you want to make? It's all important.

3. Identify three things on your list that you feel you can achieve in the next twelve months.

Here is where you start to narrow your focus to what is achievable on a more immediate basis. As you go through your business plan, these twelve-month goals should be included where appropriate.

4. Identify the one item on your list that will have the most impact on your life.

This becomes your beacon. Take that beacon and ask yourself *why*. Why is that one item so important to you? It's true that when the *why* is clear, the *how* gets easy. What is the strength of your *why*? You're reading this book to learn *how*. Again, how can you competitor-proof your clients? How can you gain their empowerment? How can you increase your refer-ability? How can you get your business to the next level, so that it serves your life, instead of the other way around? While doing this exercise, don't forget the *why*. This is where leadership emerges.

Norman Schwarzkopf once said, "When it comes to leadership, people always follow character first, strategy second." We'll never trivialize your strategy, the *how* of your business. The character—who you are and the person you've become—is the *why*. The *why* is a key reason your team works with you toward your goals and the major reason your clients choose you.

This mindset also keeps you focused on your legacy. We understand that not everyone gets as excited about this as we do and we know that countless people have achieved great things without going through a goal-setting process. We also know that everyone at some point has to ponder one of the two "coulds" in life—what "could be" or what "could have been." Goals give us anticipation and focus so that we can see beyond the present to a bigger picture. It's a magnetic force. As we've said, we believe that there is an invisible ally out there who helps us become unstoppable if we will just visualize and imagine what we want to unfold in our lives.

But let's tie this back to your company. You have given a lot to your business, and it's time for your business to give a little back. The entrepreneurial precept is true—your business is supposed to serve your life, not the other way around. By regularly taking the time to go through this exercise and answer these questions, you will re-calibrate your approach and strengthen your resolve to ensure that you achieve exactly what you want to achieve. As Lily Tomlin said, "I always wanted to be someone. I guess I should have been more specific."

Remember

» Go through a goal-setting exercise at regular intervals in your life and include these questions for clarity and perspective.

Take Action Now! (Week 4)

» Print the Goal-Setting Worksheets found on our website, **www.paretoplatform.com**, and take the time to answer the questions.

» Visit **www.breakthroughbusinessdevelopment.com** to see updates and insights from the field on this topic and others.

PART 3:
ACTIVITIES:
YOUR BUSINESS
DEVELOPMENT ACTIONS
(WEEKS 5–12)

CHAPTER 8
ESTABLISH A CLIENT-CENTERED CODE OF CONDUCT USING DART

Excellence is a habit, not an act. We are what we repeatedly do.

Aristotle

When you go through the Target- and Goal-Setting process, a major portion of your wish list will undoubtedly reflect your productivity goals. Now it is time to identify the specific activities that will turn your productivity objectives into reality.

The Law of Cause and Effect reminds us that if we want our productivity levels to increase, we must focus on the activities that garner the greatest return on our investment of effort. It bears repeating that eighty percent of your productivity stems from twenty percent of your activities. Most entrepreneurs make about eighty percent of their income, every day, in about an hour. We're not trivializing the eighty percent of activities that garner you only twenty percent of your return, though. After all, they're important; every-thing matters and everything you do affects everything else. The key, however, is to focus on the activities that matter most.

We continually see companies of all shapes and sizes that seem to only get things right in areas that don't really matter that much. An airline may boast about how many awards their in-flight magazine wins, yet have the lowest on-time arrival and departure rating in the business. Some businesses focus on how nice their office looks, yet they are abysmal at client service. Who cares if they have nice furniture and fancy golf shirts? At the end of the day, it doesn't matter.

We've seen a business owner who was obsessed with saving mon-ey, yet treated his sales and service people like second-class citizens. He would spend one dollar on something worth two (something he didn't really need anyway) and brag about how savvy he was as a buyer. Yet he would berate and belittle his sales crew (the engine of his company), resent that he had to pay out commissions, and then wonder why his business stalled. Talk about majoring in minor concerns. He would be better to make a quick decision to spend two dollars on something worth one (but that he really needed) to then free himself up to ensure that his sales and service staff were happy and that the departments were running like finely oiled machines.

We're not suggesting that you be casual about how you spend money. That would make about as much sense as buying retail and selling wholesale. What we are saying is that we don't want you to get the small things right at the expense of the big things. We sug-gest that tasks like making purchases take a backseat to the most important aspect of your business: driving productivity and creating positive client experiences that exceed expectations.

This has never been more important than today because client expectations have never been lower. Think about airlines. What are your expectations when you travel? Most of us are just hoping for same-day service. We don't expect much. We just hope things will be uneventful. That client mindset exists throughout virtually all business sectors. It is a rare exception to experience a business relationship where the vendor really tries to get it right. If that's the case, we should really strive to achieve mastery in order to set ourselves apart from the competition. In other words, the most important activities we can engage in are the activities that have the greatest impact on client acquisition and satisfaction.

To that end, we are continually reminding our coaching and consulting clients to be unreasonably time- and capital-efficient, with a particular emphasis on time, because contrary to the old cliché, time is NOT money—it's much more valuable than money. You can make more money, but all of us have just twenty-four hours in a day. When you spend your time, it's gone. Being mindful of this is what gives effective entrepreneurs the winning edge. They are unreasonable with how they invest their time.

As a reminder, the winning edge suggests that the disparity in abilities between the best and the rest are often very small. The disparities in rewards, however, between the best and rest are huge. You see it in all walks of life.

A great example of this is professional sports. The winner of a golf tournament plays four rounds of golf and wins a million dollars. When you break it down, based on cause and effect, if that golfer averaged seventy shots per round for a total score of 280, it means he made close to $3,600 every time he hit the golf ball. Not bad. Look at the leader board for #10 on the list. He or she made about $100,000. Was #1 ten times better than #10? Clearly not. That #10 averaged about seventy-two shots per round, which means only eight strokes separated the two players. However, #10 made close to $350 per shot. Still not bad, but compared to the winner, the productivity was dramatically different.

Like the winning athlete, top entrepreneurs are not ten times smarter, they don't work ten times harder, they don't spend ten times more on marketing. They have the winning edge and we are convinced it starts with this next point.

When we work with an entrepreneur in the area of activities, our first goal is to help him or her establish a code of conduct. A code of conduct is simply a pre-determined array of habits that the entrepreneur relies on daily. Now please understand that, in our view at least, there is a profound difference between being disciplined and habitually doing what's important. We're not the most disciplined people when it comes to business, but we do have some good habits.

We see people who are more disciplined than us all the time. And this extends beyond just the business environment. Perhaps it's someone who, for example, is so disciplined when it comes to health that they won't eat steak or drink wine because they believe it will help them live longer. (It must just seem longer.) Obviously, if eating steak and drinking wine becomes a habit, then it can become an issue. But remember what Ben Franklin said, "Wine is proof that God loves us."

We know someone who spends a great deal of time cleaning his garage—a lot of time! Granted, his garage is much cleaner than either of ours and that's great, if it works for him. But what does he sacrifice in order to achieve something that doesn't ultimately matter that much? (He spends more time being organized than we do looking for a hammer.)

Okay, so maybe we're just being petty, trying to rationalize why we like wine and why we don't like to clean the garage. It's not that we're lazy; we just don't want to do something minor if it means something major will be sacrificed in the process. (Yes, drinking wine is major!)

Let's bring this back to more of a business focus. At the end of a seminar we conducted a while back, a very professional and soft-spoken financial advisor approached us and spoke about how refreshing it had been to hear us talk about the importance of developing good habits. He'd found that other fancy marketing strategies produced, at best, modest results. He then handed us a small booklet distributed by National Association of Insurance and Financial Advisors in Washington, D.C. The booklet was the transcript of a speech presented by Albert Gray at the 1940 National Association of Life Underwriters convention. The title of the speech was The Common Denominator for Success.

We read the booklet. Mr. Gray's first point struck a chord. The author described the impact of realizing that the secret he was trying to discover lay not simply in what men and women did to be successful but also in what made them do it. He came to understand that the secret of success lies in habits formed. Successful people habitually do things unsuccessful people don't do.

As business development consultants, we have seen firsthand that those achieving success in business have developed and consistently practice simple habits and rituals. They stay true to those habits long enough for the results to compound and take on a life of their own. Habits compound just like money does. Think about the Rule of Seventy-Two, which when applied states that if you divide an interest rate you are earning on an investment into seventy-two it will tell you how long it takes for your investment to double in value. (So ten percent means about seven years or so.) Compounding is a beautiful thing. We want you to focus on what matters most and develop good habits, and then wait patiently for your habits to compound in the way of measurable productivity.

The following concept is a time-tested framework for developing a professional code of conduct. As you can tell, we're big on acronyms. We like them because they package a concept neatly, are thought-provoking, and best of all they are memorable. The acronym here is the word DART. Each of the four letters in DART represents a cornerstone of your professional code of conduct and, as you will see, contains a variety of sound business development habits.

Deserve
Ask
Reciprocate
Thank

We'll devote the next four chapters to these cornerstones.

Remember

  »   Begin the process of creating a culture for habits and rituals within your business. Ensure that everyone on your team has created and sticks to a Code of Conduct consisting of the most essential activities.

Take Action Now! (Week 5)

  »   Print the Code of Conduct Worksheets found on our website, **www.paretoplatform.com**, to ensure you are relying on good habits.

  »   Visit **www.breakthroughbusinessdevelopment.com** to see updates and insights from the field on this topic and others.

CHAPTER 9

DESERVE

The marketplace rewards us because we earn and deserve, not because we want or need.

Business Maxim

The D in DART is the foundation of it all, and it stands for *deserve*. You must deserve every single thing you want your client to do for you. Do you *deserve* their loyalty? Do you *deserve* their empowerment? Do you *deserve* their endorsements? If you're in the knowledge-for-profit business, such as consulting, you have to ask yourself, do I *deserve* the fees I charge? In other words, am I fee-worthy?

Look at the word *deserve*. If you split the word between the first *e* and the *s* you are reminded that the word originates from the Latin words *to serve*. An unwavering commitment by you and your team to impeccable proactive and reactive client service is the foundation to achieving client loyalty, empowerment and endorsements.

What's interesting is that when we have a conversation with a client on this topic, more often than not they tell us that they have this area well under control. Upon closer inspection, however, we discover that some crucial refinements can and must be made. For example, one business owner told us that service wasn't an issue for him because his clients never called to complain about anything. "Everything must be fine," he said. He felt that no news was good news, yet after one client survey we revealed that very few clients were anything more than merely satisfied. In other words, his deliverables were acceptable but not great. Some mentioned a few negative issues to us but they couldn't be bothered to complain to our client.

Ultimately you can never achieve perfection in terms of your proactive and reactive service deliverables. There is always room for improvement. And yet you can never be satisfied.

First and foremost, we all need to be reminded that client relationships are never static. You have to think of trust and loyalty the same way you do exercise. Sometimes you just have to keep up with the natural decline. Our bodies, at a certain age, naturally and slowly start to slide. We have to continually fight this off with exercise. Nothing strengthens without effort. With relationships, there exists a law called the Law of Familiarity, which states that the longer a relationship exists, the more things tend to be taken for granted over time. An entrepreneur with a sense of relationship entitlement has a mindset of entrenched success and is therefore vulnerable. Loyalty fatigue sets in with clients and they gradually become more open to other options.

Top companies understand that service is marketing. Even a negative situation, when handled well, can lead to a memorable experience for a client. The Ritz-Carlton Hotel & Resorts chain is legendary is this regard. There, staff at all lines of contact with clients are empowered to dazzle guests at every opportunity.

Not too long ago, one of our company spokesmen was at a Ritz-Carlton hotel in California for a conference. While killing time waiting for his designated speaking time (the much coveted after-lunch slot), he was outside on a balcony looking at the ocean and proceeded to sit down on a window sill to soak up the view—a window sill that had just been freshly painted! Saying to himself, "That didn't feel right..." he stood up and realized that his entire backside was coated in yellow paint. He looked down and saw the "Just Painted" sign that had blown off and was now on the ground, and then looked at his watch and realized that he was due to speak in about fifteen minutes. He thought to himself, "This should be interesting."

He then ran downstairs to a small shop where, among other things, they sold a modest array of clothing. Not saying a word, he showed the staff his new paint job. Mortified, they sprang into action. The mannequin, fortunately, was wearing a pair of black pants that were the perfect size for our guy. Within minutes, like a SWAT maneuver, the painted pants were off and the mannequin's pants were on and being hemmed. Five minutes later our spokesman was off to deliver his presentation.

Now that alone would be enough, but the story doesn't end there. After his speech, our guy went back to the store to say thanks and to pick up his painted pants. There, waiting for him, were perfectly cleaned pants, pressed and hung in a travel bag ready to go. A Ritz staff member said, "We're terribly sorry, sir. Thanks for being so pleasant and understanding." We will be telling this story for years to come. And in the process, Ritz Carlton will be receiving some much deserved praise from (yet another) group of flag-waving advocates.

And that is really part of the point. We often ask an entrepreneur to tell us what they feel is undermining their refer-ability. Think about it—what is holding your clients back from sending the quality and quantity of referrals you want? Are you refer-able?

When it comes to trust, your clients need to know exactly how it will reflect on them when they refer a friend to you. If your client has any uncertainty, if there is a mystery of any kind, as easy as it is to make an endorsement, it's still easier not to. In the case of some of your clients, they just don't want to take the risk that comes from referring a friend. What if things don't work out? Like the old saying suggests, no good deed goes unpunished.

This brings us to an interesting example. We've already established that we like wine. We especially like finding the gems—the twenty-dollar bottle of wine that should be a hundred dollars. (There is enough hundred-dollar wine that should be twenty dollars.)

Anyway, we were in Montreal at a restaurant and we came across a fantastic bottle of wine that knocked our socks off. When we got home, we told everybody who would listen, "If you find this wine, buy as much as you can!" A month later, we ran across a friend and asked him if he'd found a bottle yet.

> **Us:** Did you find that wine?
> **Friend:** Yes.
> **Us:** Did you like it?
> **Friend:** It was okay.
> **Us:** Okay??? (shocked) Did you let it breathe like we told you?
> **Friend:** No.
> **Us:** What do you eat with it?
> **Soon-to-be-former friend:** Cinnamon buns. (sheepishly)
> **Us:** Okay, you are officially off the list!

Now, we're talking about a twenty-dollar bottle of wine. We endorse it to a friend who proceeds to act on our advice and is less than dazzled. Now we feel bad, even though he didn't do with it what we'd suggested.

Take it up a notch to a substantial business endorsement. Is a client going to introduce a friend to you if he or she isn't absolutely convinced the friend will come back with glowing reviews? Not often, anyway. You need to create an atmosphere where your clients are so dazzled by your conduct that they feel no hesitation in encouraging others to experience it, too.

We can remember one client who had a bit of a struggle with this. He asked clients for names of people they felt could use his services. Some of his clients complied and provided names and phone numbers. Our client, prior to working with us, would call up the friends of his clients and say, "You'll never guess what your buddy has done to you—he's told me to chase you down..." And so it would go. Our client laughed when he proudly told us this and proceeded to say that most people laughed on the other line when he said it and occasionally some of the friends became clients.

Needless to say, we transformed this approach for him. We told him that not only was that a lousy way to start a relationship, it was also a tactic that we felt hurt him more than helped him. Again, it's not what you say to people that matters, it's what they hear. We were adamant that this approach reflected badly on him to both the friend and the referring client.

The following will outline how you can address the issue of clarity with your clients so that they feel you deserve their loyalty and endorsements.

CREATE A CLIENT SERVICE MATRIX

With most of what we suggest, when it comes to service, you must decide to what degree each class of client will receive it. A Client Service Matrix goes a long way in this regard.

Sit down with your team and list all of your client service deliverables. Include everything—call rotations, newsletters, review meetings, planning sessions—every single form of service you provide, right down to thank you cards. Use the template on our website to get the process started. It is an incredibly revealing process and you and your team will probably be amazed when you see this sheet of paper listing everything you do.

Beside that list, make a column for accountability. Who takes care of each of those services? Who does it? Put the initials of the person responsible for implementation next to the task itself. For instance, if you are a consultant and you have a meeting with a prospective client, do you yourself confirm that meeting? (When was the last time your dentist called you to confirm your appointment? Did the dentist call, or did the receptionist?) The column is about accountability and serves as a gentle reminder to ensure that you focus on your core activities and only on the activities that are the best use of your time. Based on the Pareto Principle, you should be performing about twenty percent of the tasks while your team is performing the remaining eighty percent. Furthermore, it ensures that you are investing eighty percent of your time on the twenty percent of your clients who generate eighty percent of the business. (Wow—that is a mouthful.)

Incidentally, this Client Service Matrix will integrate with your Organizational Chart and Procedures Manual.

Beside the accountability column, dedicate a column to your Triple-A clients. Triple-A clients get a check mark for every service deliverable you provide. They deserve it. In your enlightened self-interest, you know that Single-A clients and every other client classification you have should not necessarily receive the same level of service as Triple-A clients do. (Double-A clients have more potential than others, so treat them like Triple-As.) There isn't enough time in the day to try to be all things to all people.

What will happen if you don't delineate the service you are providing based on client classification? Well, here's the risk you run: The eighty percent of clients who generate twenty percent of your revenue will end up doing most of the referring. This is an extension of what is called the Jevons Paradox, which states that sometimes a solution to a problem can eventually make the problem worse.

In this case, if you take our Referral Process and apply it without the focus of a Client Service Matrix, you will increase the quantity of referrals you receive but not the quality. Now there are exceptions to every rule, but most clients tend to refer people pretty much like themselves. If your goal is to replicate your Triple-A clients, you must blanket them with eighty percent of your attention. To punctuate this point, the Client Service Matrix is designed to ensure that you never spend excessive time with the eighty percent of your clients who generate twenty percent of your revenue at the expense of your most deserving twenty percent—especially your Triple-A clients. We're not being harsh or elitist; we're simply asking you to guard your time.

STIR THE POT WITH A NINETY-DAY CALL ROTATION

Incidentally, at the very top of your list of service deliverables for Triple-A clients must be the ninety-day call rotation. Simply put, if you have 107 existing and potential Triple-A clients right now, it means that you will be calling two or three of them every business day over the course of the next ninety days (each client will receive one call within this period). This is an absolutely essential habit to create and stick with.

You aren't calling to be the bearer of any profound news, nor are you trying to sell anything. You are simply touching base with your favorite clients to demonstrate that you appreciate them and are thinking about them. As you are speaking with each of them, you have his or her FORM profile open and are investing the conversation into the rest of the relationship. If you have good chemistry with the client, chances are that in a twenty-minute conversation, fifteen minutes will be focused on their Family, Occupation and Recreational interests, with just a few minutes focused on your Message.

We could parade a number of entrepreneurs through your office who would tell you, "The call rotation is what I really get paid to do." We have a client on the West Coast who starts his day very early and wraps each day up at about two o'clock and takes off every Friday. His business runs like a Swiss watch. As he leaves each day, one of his assistants hands him a sheet of paper with the names of two clients and their numbers. He calls them from the car on his way home. He says, "Half the time they're not even there so I just leave a voice mail." What does he say to them? "Hey, how's it going? I was just thinking about you and checking in to see how things are." And, using his FORM information, he makes an inquiry or two. Often, his clients call him back, thanking him for calling. He continues, "The other half of the time, I'm sitting in my driveway for twenty minutes talking to a great client." How much time does he spend talking about his Message? "Almost never," he said. "Very little. It's mostly Family, Occupation, Recreation." It's simple. It's powerful. And it's easy to do. But if it's so simple, so powerful and so easy to do, why doesn't everybody do it? Because it's even easier not to. It's easy to think there are more important things to do.

The problem for us, of course, is that this kind of advice isn't profound either. It doesn't make for a very compelling seminar or coaching module. It's not as if someone says to us, "Give me one good idea!" to which we reply, "Er, call your clients!" to which our student says, "Okay, whoa, slow down—that is powerful. Let me jot that down. C-a-l-l m-y c-l-i-e-n-t-s..." It is such a basic concept that it is often overlooked or dismissed. Take the advice of Vince Lombardi, who said, "The best in any field of endeavor are brilliant at the basics."

Nothing could be more important than consistently reaching out to touch base with your Triple-A clients. In fact, if all you do as a result of reading this book (if you aren't already doing so) is habitually contact your Triple-A clients using FORM, we'll feel accomplished and proud that we had an impact.

If you don't reach out and continually "stir the pot," you run the risk of essentially saying that you take your Triple-A clients for granted. If a relationship gets neglected, it will get stale. Ever heard the saying, Absence makes the heart grow fungus? You're conspicuous by your absence and in the process you undermine your ability to competitor-proof your clients, gain their full empowerment and stimulate good referrals. Incidentally, if you have the capacity, it's not a bad idea to empower your team to contact select Double-A, Single-A and other clients as part of a call rotation to try to uncover untapped opportunities.

Remember

- » Strive to be all things to some people—those "some people" are your Triple-A and Double-A clients.

Take Action Now! (Week 5)

- » Use the actionable templates found on our website, **www.paretoplatform.com**, to create your own Client Service Matrix and to make the call rotation a habit.
- » Visit **www.breakthroughbusinessdevelopment.com** to see updates and insights from the field on this topic and others.

CHAPTER 10
ASK

You're not asking people to buy things from you, you are asking them to buy into a relationship based on trust and mutual fit.

Duncan MacPherson and David Miller

ASKING STARTS THE RECEIVING PROCESS

Once you are on track in terms of creating and deploying a Client Service Matrix, you will *deserve* client loyalty, empowerment and endorsements. You then move to the A in DART, which stands for *ask*. You must *ask* your clients and prospects to do what you want. Everything you want your clients and prospective clients to do, you must *ask* them to do. But here is the caveat: Based on creating a professional code of conduct, you must examine *how* you ask them. Again, you can never project a need to your clients. You must project your value so that they can determine what is in it for them.

Business owners who *chase* clients ask differently than business owners who *attract* clients. We want you to attract high-caliber clients and therefore we are asking you to closely scrutinize all the ways you *ask* people to do things, to ensure that it conveys a benefit to them.

Before you start analyzing how to ask for referrals and more business, it's important to get a sense for how your clients perceive you. A great place to start is to ask key Triple-A clients to attend a Client Advisory Council (CAC). This proven and incredibly revealing process enables you to get feedback on your overall approach. If you want to improve the way you deliver your messages and services, *ask* the people at the receiving end of what you deliver. Mark Twain said it best: "A customer is the only critic whose opinion really counts." So *ask* them how you are doing.

Logistically speaking, the CAC is nothing more than a casual gathering of a small group of your best clients around a boardroom table. (We've put the entire turnkey process on our website. Everything you'll need to get your group together, what to say when they are together with you, and how to say thanks after the session has taken place, can be implemented in a sequential and predictable manner.)

We could tell you some staggering stories. One client we proposed this to was initially quite skeptical but eventually agreed to try it. We said, "Make a list of your fifteen favorite clients. It might help if we told you to imagine that you had to give all your clients away and were allowed to keep only fifteen. Call them up and say, 'I take my business very seriously but I don't want to get complacent. I know I can always raise the bar and the best way to do that is to ask the people who receive our service. Next Saturday I'm getting together with a small group of my clients and I will ask you all an array of important questions. Your feedback will be crucial to me and I will strive to take action on it as soon as possible.'" He called the fifteen, and fourteen of them were flattered, while one was going to be out of town.

He got together with these fourteen people for what he thought was going to be a one-hour meeting. Three hours later when they finished, he was blown away. He asked them all the questions provided in the agenda within our process. For example, he asked this question about refer-ability (question #7 on our agenda): "Have I earned the right for you to feel comfortable and confident enough to introduce a friend or family member to me? Yes or no?" One of his clients said to him, "I didn't even know you took referrals." He didn't ask for a referral. He just put it out there and it opened a very important dialogue about the concept of referrals. (As you will see, this is a huge philosophical departure in our approach as compared to others'—you don't need to ask for referrals, you simply need to professionally and attractively communicate that you accept them.)

Anyway, his CAC cost him a few hundred dollars. Big spender, right? He did it in his boardroom, provided doughnuts and coffee and gave everybody a pen. He was so amazed by the reaction that he held another CAC less than a year later. This one cost him about $2,200. In his boardroom, he had a follow-up conversation with the fourteen and told them, "Here's what's happened since we had our meeting, here's the adjustments we've made. Thank you." After a two-hour meeting they were whisked away to the Rogers Centre (formerly the Sky Dome) in Toronto for a baseball game.

He was so completely amazed at the now-advocate status of these fourteen people that he was inspired to take the third session to an even higher level. The third CAC cost him $10,000! If you can believe it, he rented a bed and breakfast in Niagara Falls for a weekend and invited the CAC members and their significant others. He spoiled them all rotten. He said to us, "The money's a drop in the bucket when you consider how much business has been generated by my Board of Directors," as he now calls them.

Some business owners worry about opening the door to negative feedback about themselves. Frankly, given these are your best clients, with whom you have good relationships, you'd hopefully already know if they had any less-than-favorable feelings for you. But it is a common concern. Some seem to think that their top clients have been dying for this chance to assemble a lynch mob to seek out some kind of revenge and then walk away with their business en masse.

Let us share with you what we've witnessed at dozens of CACs. When your clients arrive, they are clear about the agenda. They know you want to hear from them how you can improve your service. They understand you think their opinion/perspective is important and worthy. When your clients show up they are already somewhat impressed.

The CAC is not a gimmick or a trick—quite the opposite, in fact. You are trying to communicate your philosophy as effectively as you can and to be completely open with your clients. You are essentially telling them, "My success is predicated on your satisfaction. Help me get a clearer understanding of what people like you expect and value. I will consider everything you tell me, and if it can be implemented, I'll do it."

Your first CAC is the proverbial tip of the iceberg. It is imperative that your council understand that you wish to meet with them at least two, perhaps three, times over the course of the next twenty-four months.

Remember

> » Make your clients the voice you listen to. No one can offer better advice for taking your business to the next level than the members of your Client Advisory Council.

Take Action Now! (Week 6)

> » Customize the turnkey Client Advisory Council campaign and templates found on our website, **www.paretoplatform.com**, and plan your first CAC right away!

> » Visit **www.breakthroughbusinessdevelopment.com** to see updates and insights from the field on this topic and others.

ASK PEOPLE TO MOVE UP YOUR LOYALTY LADDER

The Client Advisory Council, at the very least, will be invaluable for enabling you to ask your clients how you are doing. In the process, your ability to competitor-proof your clients will increase. You now need to shift gears to determine how you can:

- ask prospective clients to do business with you
- ask existing customers to become fully empowering clients
- ask clients to become referral-generating advocates

We'll say it again: It is essential that you scrutinize your current approach to ensure that when you ask your client to do something it is positioned as a service to them rather than as a benefit to you. The way you ask can actually undermine your results because of how the client perceives you in terms of professionalism.

Let's talk for a moment about how you deal with prospective clients and what mindset you have in terms of improving your persuasive impact. When a prospective client actually decides to do business with you and comes on board, who views that as an accomplishment? Do you view it as an accomplishment because you closed the sale, or do they view it as an accomplishment because they qualified to work with you? If you ask nine out of ten entrepreneurs, they are the ones celebrating when a new customer comes on board. Nowhere in the process does the prospect have to convince the entrepreneur that there is a good fit. The entrepreneur is doing all of the convincing. And for that reason, those entrepreneurs are not very attractive, let alone referable. Why? Because salespeople use a sales process and consultants use a fit process. This is the prime distinction between chasing new clients and attracting them. It goes beyond the instant gratification of making a sale. Think of the long-term impact. It is much easier to refer a friend to a consultant than it is to refer them to a salesperson.

Before you dismiss this concept, let us remind you that there is a profound difference between salesmanship and stewardship. Salespeople focus on the transaction and primarily sell the message, while consultative professionals focus on the relationship and strive to establish a mutually beneficial fit.

It is for this reason that we tell our coaching and consulting clients NOT to attempt to "close the sale" when they meet a prospective client for the first time. Think about it. The hidden agenda of most sales-driven businesspeople who meet prospective clients for the first time is to try to close them. (And let's be honest, most prospective clients expect to be sold to, which explains why they are so guarded at the beginning of a meeting.) We say you should have no hidden agenda and here's why. A "sales process" creates external motivation—you motivate the person to take action. External motivation is temporary; it has the lasting value of a caffeine rush. A "fit process" builds self-motivation—the prospective client comes to his or her own conclusions and feels no buyer's remorse or mixed feelings.

Based on that reality, your goal is to conduct yourself in a manner that contrasts your approach favorably to his or her current provider. That favorable contrast does not come from your ability to close them using salesmanship, as counterintuitive as that may sound.

You actually have three goals when meeting with a prospective client for the first time. If you achieve these three goals you will dramatically increase your persuasive impact over that of a salesperson.

Goal #1: Validation. When you meet a prospective client who's been introduced to you by an existing client, at the very least you want that prospect to go back to your existing client and validate the introduction, informing the existing client he or she was right to recommend you. And just then, what's happened? The referral tap has been turned on, flat out. Your existing client will continue to refer you—there is no mystery and he or she knows exactly how the endorsement will reflect back on him or her.

Goal #2: Contrast. As mentioned a moment ago, as prospects are engaged in a conversation with you, they begin comparing your approach to the other approaches encountered. This is referred to as the Contrast Principle. As they start contrasting you favorably, they become predisposed to wanting to do business with you. This is essential if you hope to break the status quo and lay to rest any uncertainty that may be swirling around in the prospective client's mind. They came in expecting to be sold but instead were exposed to a consultative process. A sense builds that it will be worth the effort to switch providers. This leads to the all-important third goal.

Goal #3: Self-Motivation. When prospective clients meet with you for the first time, a combination of two emotions exists: anticipation and apprehension. To a lesser extent there's anticipation, which exists because they are thinking of the upside that could come from making a switch or all the benefits that could come from taking action. If they were referred to you, they obviously heard good things about you and they want to believe that the comments are true and accurate. To a greater extent there's apprehension, which stems from their fear of making a bad decision, fear of change and, of course, fear of being sold. People today are naturally skeptical and guarded when they meet with a new vendor or service provider for the first time, because past experience tells them that the hidden agenda of that person is to sell them something. Again, they are expecting to be sold to. So, if that fear exists, why feed it? Again, keep the Law of Attraction in mind. The more you push, the more you repel. Stop chasing and start attracting. With our process, you will literally see the apprehension melt away as the prospective client realizes you are a consultative professional.

Here is the process:

STEP 1: ALWAYS USE AN AGENDA

After the pleasantries at the beginning of the initial meeting, slide a formal agenda across the table (there are samples on our website). This powerful tool tells the person that you value his or her time and that you have a process to follow. As you will see in the templates, the agenda includes the prospective client's name, as well as the date and time of the meeting. It is then followed by a series of bullets that itemize the points you wish to discuss throughout the meeting, such as:

- Meeting Overview
- Getting to Know Each Other
- An Introduction to My Firm
- An Overview of My Credentials and Mindset
- What's Important to You?
- The Uniqueness of My Approach
- Is There a Fit?

It is a good idea to provide the prospective client with a notepad and pen to use throughout the meeting and then to mention that you will be forwarding an Executive Summary of the meeting a day later to help him or her digest what you've discussed.

STEP 2: HAVE NO HIDDEN AGENDA

As the prospective client is scanning your agenda, make a powerful statement about your professional code of conduct by using a personalized variation of this statement:

Right up front, I appreciate that you made the time to meet with me today. I know you are a busy person and there are a number of things you could be doing instead of meeting with me and I don't take that lightly. I know you wanted to meet with me to get to know me and my firm and to assess our credentials and competencies and that is what I want to convey in this initial meeting. I wanted to meet with you to get to know you and to determine if we'll have good chemistry over the lifetime of this potential relationship. And because a decision like this is important to both of us, at the end of this meeting, no one has to make any decisions or commitments. We'll both step back and digest what we've discussed. You can take some time to determine if you feel we are a good fit for you. I'll meet with my team and discuss your situation and determine the same. We'll contact you in forty-eight hours to tell you if we feel we are good fit for each other. Is that fair?

With a personalized version of this approach you will have diffused, disarmed and melted the apprehension away. Think about it. Put yourself in the prospect's shoes. What was he expecting, based on past experience? He was expecting you to sell to him and instead you took a completely different, low-key and professional approach.

If you are having a tough time believing in this method, let us tell you that after years of dealing with countless consulting clients who have transitioned to this forthright and professional consultative approach, only once has an entrepreneur called us to say that he contacted a prospective client forty-eight hours later only to be told by the prospective client that he was going with somebody else. And this happened only because the entrepreneur completely deviated from our approach.

On the other side of the equation, how many entrepreneurs have called us to say that they followed this process but at the end of the meeting the prospective client tried to close the entrepreneur? Countless times. Prospective clients will become so self-motivated that they will say things like, "I don't need to think about it" or "Everything my friend told me about you is bang on—I'm ready to get started right now." You will be amazed. In fact, at a recent seminar we were conducting on this very topic, we were literally interrupted by a client of ours who was in attendance. He stood up and informed the crowd, "He's right, this works." Our reply was simple. "This works because it's right. It is professional and it sets the relationship on the right track from the beginning." We'll say it again. How you start a relationship has a profound impact on how it unfolds in the years to come. We're not saying it's a universal approach, but we do ask you to determine how it can affect you and to customize it accordingly.

So what would you do if the prospective client said, "Look, I'm a busy guy. I don't need to think about it. Everything my buddy said about you has been confirmed in my mind. My current provider has let me down several times yet keeps coming back to the well when it serves him. I'm done! Plus, I'm going out of town tomorrow. I want to take care of this right now"? How would you respond? Would you be consistent and congruent?

We tell our clients to maintain the integrity of the approach by saying this:

> Mr. Client, I appreciate your enthusiasm. I really do. However, this is a process we follow because this is an important decision for both of us. If that is how you feel, I don't think your enthusiasm will fade in forty-eight hours. Take some time and let me meet with my team. This is a process we follow. We'll work around your schedule.

That said, in extreme examples there are prospective clients who press you quite aggressively to take them on as clients. You can only deviate from the process under one condition: They are a good fit and perfectly meet your Triple-A Ideal Client Profile.

For example, let's say the prospect has been referred to you by a great client and at the end of the initial meeting he is relentless about becoming a client. You have to qualify why you are caving in.

> I wouldn't ordinarily do this but you are a very good friend of one of our favorite clients and also you perfectly match our Ideal Client Profile. Your desire to take action based on our areas of expertise is perfect. Your attitude is completely consistent with ours and you've demonstrated you think of yourself as an advocate. So, we're prepared to make the exception.

What did we do? We qualified the changed rules of engagement based on an existing client endorsement and the Triple-A profile. Don't just cave in. It would be like saying it was just a big smoke screen and a test to see if they're serious. Integrity, consistency and rules of engagement must be omnipresent. Furthermore, when a relationship starts, you can't be the only person who gets excited. You want the prospective client to feel just as accomplished, just as good about coming on board with you, as you feel about having him come on board. You're looking for a good fit, you're thinking of the lifetime value of the relationship, and he's buying *into* something, not buying something.

Think of stewardship, not salesmanship. Salesmanship can get you new business, but stewardship is far more attractive. By following this process, you will fast-track all new relationships to advocate status and effectively create the desired level of scarcity.

SCARCITY CREATES ABUNDANCE

The issue of scarcity does not just apply to prospective clients but rather it is an all-encompassing mindset pertaining to your entire clientele. Regardless, the process outlined above is essential for creating scarcity from the outset of all your client relationships.

In developing scarcity, as you continually work to evolve your business, you would do well to adhere to one of the basic and most fundamental laws of business: supply and demand. This is economics 101. The *supply* is your availability. Your clients provide the *demand* by requesting your time and services. Your available time is finite. Excess demand creates competition among your clients for your time.

By limiting your availability, you are increasing the demand for your time and your perceived value. You are able to differentiate between the clients who *deserve* to see you face to face and the ones who *want* to see you for whatever reason.

So you have a decision to make: Will you project abundance or scarcity in your approach? Sure, there is a place for abundance in business—email didn't do away with paper, because people began printing their emails, while video rental actually increased movie theater attendance for a while. And sometimes abundance of one thing leads to increased demand for another.

The point is that an Alchemy Effect can be triggered by an abundance and growth business model. And it's not always literal or obvious either. The increase in the consumption of wine and coffee has led to a boom in sales for teeth whitening. And as the world becomes increasingly mobile and wireless, the sale of batteries has gone through the roof. One need fulfilled can lead to another need being created—an Alchemy Effect. Necessity really is the mother of invention and that is what makes our economy so fascinating.

But as an entrepreneur, you have to at least consider the risks in being seduced by the vast perceived opportunities of continual growth based on supply and demand and its relationship with your distribution model and capacity to serve.

As an example, we know an exceptional golf instructor who was always in demand and in the process was burning himself out. He decided to drastically increase his fees and in short order found himself in a position to actually turn away even more business. He was in even higher demand because he was perceived as being an even better instructor. After all, with fees that high he must be a great teacher, right? In time, he became very selective and began attracting referrals from his very best clients. And often, the quality of the people referred to him was very comparable to his best clients.

A discipline like this can result in you spending time with your Triple-A clients who, as you know, keep you in business. The alternative is to supply too much of your time to those clients who don't contribute very much to the bottom line (the eighty percent who generate twenty percent of the business).

People typically want what they can't have. Look at the world today. The things that people place a high value on are those things that are not mass-produced, nor are they readily available. They are rare—the availability is scarce, not abundant. Seldom do we encounter business owners who attempt to create scarcity. More often than not, entrepreneurs provide their time to anyone who will listen. Unfortunately, it is the business owner who ultimately pays the price for not limiting his or her access.

By applying the scarcity principle, you will attract the clients you want and you will consequently have more time for what we believe to be most important—your family and the pursuit of happiness outside of your business. Remember, optics and perceptions play a role in your success. How you are perceived is something you have to be mindful of. (Does a car really drive better after a car wash? It feels like it, doesn't it? That is the perception.)

We'll leave you with this example. You're walking along a street and you see a sun-faded sign in the window of a dentist's office that reads *Dr. Phil McCavity is accepting new patients.* Are you attracted to this dentist, who after years in practice is still taking strangers off the street? What does he use in there, pliers and rum? Contrast this to a friend telling you about how great her dentist is. As she raves about him, you suggest that you should go and see him, to which your friend replies, "Well, you would love him but he does have a three-month waiting list. Do you want me to call his office to get you on the list?"

The bottom line is this: If you want to improve your persuasive impact, especially with high-caliber clients, stop selling! Use a fit process rather than a sales process and you will improve your client retention, gain a greater portion of what is often referred to as "wallet share" (meaning your clients will buy more from you) and attract a higher quality and quantity of referrals from your best clients. Many businesspeople view this as a dichotomy, but again, that is the difference between chasing and attracting. (Speaking of a dichotomy, did you know that the state of Tennessee is the largest producer of both bibles and whiskey in America?)

Incidentally, with prospective clients you can also take the opportunity to plant the referral seed before they have even become a client. When you are discussing issues prompted by the agenda bullet The Uniqueness of My Approach, you can say this:

> Mr. Prospective Client, there are several value-added services
> I provide that my clients really find to be of value. One of
> them is that I make myself available to act as a sounding
> board for friends and family members of my clients. Should
> we decide to work together, I will outline that process for you.

You didn't ask for a referral or look needy. You presented it as a service and planted the seed. As you will see later when we explain our Referral Process, that seed-planting strategy is an invaluable step. (By the way, be prepared for prospective clients to wonder aloud who they should introduce to you before you've even decided to work together. It happens often with our clients!)

Remember

> » When meeting with prospective clients, use an agenda and
> have no hidden agenda.

Take Action Now! (Week 6)

> » Use the Sample Agendas and the "Is There a Fit?" scripting
> found on our website, **www.paretoplatform.com**.
>
> » Visit **www.breakthroughbusinessdevelopment.com** to see
> updates and insights from the field on this topic and others.

CONVERTING CUSTOMERS INTO FULLY EMPOWERING CLIENTS

We've already established that customers are great prospects. So, allow us to ask you this question: Is there a chance, based on the Loyalty Ladder, that you have customers who are not fully aware of everything you do and provide? Chances are that the answer is yes, and if so, your MVPs are not just friends and family members of your clients, but are also your existing customers. How do you ask someone to become a client instead of just a customer? How do you communicate your full array of offerings? It begins with your communications about your business being as forthright, clear and precise as possible. All of your products and services should be conveyed as a service to your clients, not as something you are trying to sell. Gaining all of a client's business stems as much from your philosophy and mindset as it does from your techniques and processes.

As mentioned earlier, when you first meet with prospective clients they are usually entering into the meeting with some level of apprehension, because not everyone referred to you by an existing client necessarily understands exactly what your services and products are. Most businesspeople will immediately focus on what prospective clients have already had conveyed to them as their principal interest, and neglect sharing their full range of offerings. Meanwhile, individuals may contact a financial advisor about an investment opportunity and not mention that they have a pressing need to re-evaluate their estate planning program.

BEING FORTHRIGHT IS REFRESHING—FOR EVERYONE!

By not introducing yourself to prospective clients properly, you miss out on a golden opportunity to set yourself apart from everyone else in your field. You may end up answering their specific questions but leave them wondering about you, your company and the other services you offer that they might one day require.

The process is simple and should be directly referred to in your agenda. Rather than launching into a sales pitch trying to satisfy one immediate need, take a few moments to create rapport and then provide some background information. Tell them a bit about yourself and explain the history and background of your company. Then give them a clear understanding of your approach and show them an outline of your full array of offerings. Your approach can be documented on a sheet of paper or in a brochure that can be provided to them for more careful perusal later on. This process should only take a few minutes, but will set the prospective client at ease and start to create a level of trust that other providers typically fail to achieve.

Many entrepreneurs have been trained to ask questions in a first meeting, and this should not be neglected. Remember, it is likely that the person you are meeting with has these questions about you and your company anyway and you have now conveniently and respectfully provided them with all the answers in an upfront and forthright manner.

FULL DISCLOSURE LIGHTS THE PATH

Once this is completed, you can begin to answer the questions necessary to uncover your client's goals and objectives and start determining what it is you provide that can serve these needs. Because you first disclose information about yourself, prospective clients feel comfortable in fully disclosing the information about their situation that you need to make the appropriate decisions. In all likelihood, you will have sparked some interest in areas that they would not have otherwise revealed to you at this time. The depth of the conversation and level of communication is always enhanced with this approach. Clients feel you have their best interest in mind and perceive your full array of offerings as a service that they can take into full consideration and utilize.

To illustrate, the financial advisor we referred to earlier is dealing with a sophisticated array of services and products that requires the ultimate level of trust. We have worked with many financial advisors to create a document called the Personal Financial Policy Statement. This document tracks exactly what services have been provided in the past, what the advisor is currently working on with the client, and outlines every service that may become applicable in the future. What it does for the client is create clarity and peace of mind. The client gets a copy of the document and can refer to it at any time.

The format is simple yet precise. An advisor using this tool often finds that the client will initiate conversations about services that the advisor provides but hasn't yet formally introduced. This tool has been proven on countless occasions to reduce the abstract or complicated elements of his or her services down to easy-to-conceptualize issues for the client. A client never goes to another provider for service that is offered by the advisor and the client often uses the tool as an example to friends and associates to brag about the services that their advisor provides. The Personal Financial Policy Statement becomes the centerpiece for all review meetings in the future and a tremendous springboard for promotional partners such as accountants, lawyers, business brokers, and so on.

We have been exposed to countless other scenarios where the full disclosure concept is applicable. One of the consultants in our office recently illustrated the universality of this principle; he has been engaged in various renovations on his home over the last couple of years. His window supplier made a recommendation to someone who allegedly could be of assistance in designing and building a new foyer for their home.

This businessperson made arrangements to come out and introduce himself. He arrived in a large truck with the name of a renovation company across it. This immediately sparked some curiosities about his company. The entrepreneur was pleasant enough but dove directly into the problem at hand. He did not tell the prospective client, our staff member, anything about himself, his company, how long his company has been in business, or anything about the services they offer.

After the meeting, which was solely focused on this one project, he left to prepare a quote, robbing himself of the opportunity to create a great first impression and missing out on numerous other opportunities. This was made abundantly clear on his second visit, when he started asking things such as who was going to do the tiling and the painting and was informed that the client had recently secured another subcontractor for that work. By taking just a few moments to talk about himself and his services at the first meeting, he would have created an entirely different impression and uncovered thousands of dollars of additional business.

By creating a document similar to the Personal Financial Policy Statement for his business that clearly defined his current services and eventually his past deliverables as well as future opportunities, he could have secured a client for the future. You have to keep in mind that people want to know what you do and want to believe in you, but they've been taught to be disbelieving. This occurs over time because so many people have positioned selling as something you do *to* someone, not *with* or *for* them. Communicate all that you do as a service and it will be interpreted in a much more favorable way. Simplify people's lives by positioning yourself as a turnkey quarterback.

When you have a professional meeting agenda that promotes full disclosure, new clients will seldom question the agenda or the information you convey. Your planning of such a presentation portrays a benefit to clients from the very beginning of the relationship. Clients are subsequently extremely receptive and accommodating. Most of us, as people, as consumers, would like all the details up front. When we get that information we tend to be accepting and appreciative.

IS IT TOO LITTLE, TOO LATE TO USE FULL DISCLOSURE WITH EXISTING CUSTOMERS?

If it is done methodically and professionally, and if it conveys a benefit, you'll be happy to know that the full disclosure approach will work like a charm in your existing relationships with customers. Yes, it takes a little longer than with new clients, but it simply proves that you should master this approach sooner rather than later. It's easy to forget that the majority of your clients do business with you because you're well-liked and respected, not because you've done anything spectacular for them. Your clients like and respect you and are thus quite receptive to a more professional way of doing things, particularly when it is delivered under the umbrella of improved and more professional client service. If you're somewhat apprehensive about how your existing clients will respond, don't worry. The feedback we hear from clients is overwhelmingly appreciative. "It's about time," our clients' clients often say.

The best way to approach an existing customer relationship is to set up a review meeting with him or her. Use an agenda with a series of bullets outlining the track you want to proceed with. As always, position the concept of full empowerment as a benefit to your client so that it isn't perceived as a sales pitch. Begin by saying something like this:

> Mr. Customer (soon to be client), as you may know, up until recently I have been growing my business steadily and have been working with a wide array of different customers. I have, however, come to the realization that I have been essentially trying to be all things to all people and in the process have hit a point of diminishing returns. By that I mean my business has hit a plateau and if I continue on this track, the level of service I can provide is sure to diminish. Furthermore, I have also come to the realization that there are a number of services I provide that many of my customers aren't aware that I offer. Clearly I've been too busy to communicate these various services effectively. So, going forward, my goal will not be to see how big I can get, but rather how small I can stay, and in the process I will strive to be all things to some people. I have created an Ideal Client Profile and I will strive to only work with clients who meet this profile.

(Explain your Triple-A profile and outline how part of the ideal client attitude is reflected by the client feeling confident in empowering you fully, rather than dabbling with a variety of suppliers.)

> Based on this, I'm hoping that if you feel confident in my abilities, going forward you will feel comfortable in empowering me fully for your entire range of needs.

(Walk the customer through your Full Disclosure document.)

> Based on that, I trust you will see the value in working with someone who focuses on a good fit with clients rather than taking any and all business that happens to present itself.

Put your Full Disclosure document in a binder along with any other documentation you feel would complement it and present it to the customer. Inform them that all future documents can be placed inside the binder and that he or she should bring it with them to future meetings. Then finish by saying,

> As your needs change, please refer to this binder and contact me to discuss them at your convenience.

Please keep this in mind if, at the moment of truth, you get cold feet about shifting from a sales process to a fit process as well as a forthright approach with full disclosure. We say that because often entrepreneurs revert back to what they know. Sure, there is a fear of rejection that comes from using traditional sales tactics, but the fear of failure when it comes to making a change is stronger. Be confident—and we say this from countless experiences with our clients who have made this transition—that assuming you are well prepared, you will feel natural and comfortable when using this, even for the first time. Keep in mind that your clients want the clarity that comes with knowing exactly what you do. If there is any mystery or uncertainty, the degree of trust you develop will have a very low ceiling.

And in case you're wondering, this is a virtually universal concept. We've seen the full spectrum in this area, ranging from the very simple to very complex. From a company that does yard maintenance and unveils a "Did You Know?" campaign explaining their complete array of services, including snow clearing and hanging Christmas lights, to an accountant who communicates his holistic array of services, the outcomes are the same—if done professionally, converting a partial customer to a fully empowering client can be surprisingly effortless and lead to rapid advocacy.

MAKING EXCEPTIONS: THE SLIPPERY SLOPE

After you have mastered this approach, it is paramount to avoid making exceptions with respect to gaining a client's complete empowerment. If you make the decision to only work with clients who deal with you exclusively, you have to stick with it and have integrity for the concept. You can't flip-flop out of convenience. Ultimately you live by the rules you set, but accepting a customer's transactional business just to make a quick sale can have its consequences. Your code of conduct is on display whenever you are in front of prospective clients, but it is also in full gear when those prospective clients leave your office. If you stick to your guns, people will respect you a great deal regardless of whether they do business with you. Eventually, the integrity of consistency gathers steam and you will find it trickling down into all corners of your business. Be faithful to this philosophy and it will come back to reward you in ways you could never have imagined.

If good chemistry exists between you and the prospective client, but the prospective client has an aversion to full empowerment because of bad experiences in the past, you may wish to employ this approach:

> I appreciate where you are coming from and I feel we are
> going to have a great relationship. Why don't we do this.
> I'll take care of your business needs to the extent with which
> you feel comfortable, now. If, in twelve months' time, I have
> demonstrated to you my ability to meet those additional
> needs in a way superior to your other providers, I am going
> to insist you empower me fully. Is that fair?

This is a bit of a sidebar, but have you ever seen an article in the newspaper announcing some new study or scientific finding that seems too obvious for words? For instance, "Experts say eating too much can make you fat!" It's funny how something so obvious can be positioned as being so profound.

Not long ago we spotted an article with groundbreaking news: People really appreciate professionalism! You probably agree this seems rather obvious, too. However, consider all the business owners who simply use a legal pad and pseudo diagnostic approach rather than a prepared agenda and full disclosure when meeting with new clients. Also, consider the vast number of clients in various market sectors who don't know everything their business providers do. Perhaps the article was indeed necessary?

To summarize, if you as a business owner have an effective way of explaining your business and if it's documented into a dedicated process, interesting things start to happen. When clients are taught details about you and your business, meetings become less of an event and more of an ongoing process that involves continuous interaction between you and your clients. You effectively teach clients that the relationship will be lifelong. Documentation of this philosophy, in tandem with written agendas, helps clients to learn all of this more quickly, and it comes across as more professional, too.

Another major benefit of this approach is that your clients can educate others about you in an intelligent and compelling manner. Clients learn to recognize when friends, family members and colleagues are dropping hints about their own business needs and it becomes easy for your clients to spot those who would benefit from your services. This last aspect is enormously important and just one more feature distinguishing your professionalism and thoroughness, and separating you from the rest of the pack.

> **Remember**
>
> » Use full disclosure to convey your full array of solutions in a way that positions full empowerment as a benefit to your customers.
>
> **Take Action Now! (Week 7)**
>
> » Use the sample Customer to Client Conversion Tool found on our website, **www.paretoplatform.com**.
>
> » Visit **www.breakthroughbusinessdevelopment.com** to see updates and insights from the field on this topic and others.

ATTRACTING A HIGHER QUALITY AND QUANTITY OF REFERRALS

By now you know how we feel about the concept of advocacy: Focusing on the lifetime value of client relationships is far more effective and fulfilling over the long haul. We feel for the salespeople out there who do anything to grab a sale with their SWAT mindset (Sell What's Available Today!). The world is littered with stories of burned-out salespeople whose motivation has eroded to irreparable levels.

We admire companies that take a long-term view. Coca-Cola applied a slightly morbid yet effective "cradle to grave" mindset by introducing a wide array of beverage options—from water to juice to soda—to ensure they had something for everyone throughout an entire lifespan. Toyota anticipated the demographic shifts and introduced Lexus to ensure that nobody "outgrew" their cars. (One could argue that Lexus has helped sell more Toyotas, too. Can't you just hear the Toyota salesperson saying, "This Camry has a Lexus engine!")

In a small business, the key to advocacy is not so much the ability to have something for everyone or to focus on multi-generation selling, but rather is in how referable you are. After all, as a famous marketing maxim says: The best people to convince others on your behalf are the people who are already convinced.

In our seminars and consultations on the topic of referrals, we show entrepreneurs that attracting a higher quality and quantity of referrals from Triple-A clients stems from using a process rather than using clever phrases or salesmanship.

Earlier, we talked about some referral fundamentals. As a refresher before we really dig into this, let us remind you of some of essential ingredients in refer-ability:

- Attracting a steady stream of referrals is a process, not an array of clever phrases and tactics.
- Referrals must be positioned as a service to your clients rather than as a favor or benefit to you. You can never look needy.
- Understand the factors that undermine your refer-ability.
- Coach clients to understand why, who, and how.

At the risk of being repetitive, and just before we unveil our process to you, it is essential that you position the concept of making yourself available to meet with a client's friend as a service you provide, rather than something you want or need. Most entrepreneurs say things like "I'm trying to grow my business and I'm always looking for new clients." In the process, they make themselves look needy. You should never bring your needs to your clients. It's not attractive. Remember, you want your clients to feel compelled to introduce a friend to you because it's in their friend's best interests, not because it's in yours.

WHAT IS UNDERMINING YOUR REFER-ABILITY?

So have you given any further thought to why your clients don't send you referrals? While we talked about some of the potential reasons earlier, there are many. Perhaps it doesn't occur to them. Perhaps there is an issue of trust.

The most important issue might be that clients are very concerned about how making an endorsement will ultimately reflect back on them. If they're not convinced that you will make them look good, they won't take the risk, which, as you will see in a moment, is why having a process is so important. When you explain your process it will give your clients clarity to the point that they know exactly what will happen when they steer a friend to you.

Before we elaborate, though, let us offer an idea to enable you to see for yourself how well your clients understand the why, who and how. Simply ask ten of your favorite clients this question at the end of your next conversation with them:

> By the way, if you don't mind me asking, when you talk
> about me to a friend, what do you say? How do you
> describe me?

Most entrepreneurs who ask their clients this question are shocked by how their clients respond. It's not clear or concise, it's not all-encompassing or accurate and it certainly isn't persuasive. Worst of all, though, if your favorite clients can't describe you to you, how can you expect that they can describe you to a friend?

Our process will enable you to coach your clients on the why/who/how. Again, your clients will know *why* they should introduce people— because they will feel they are doing their friends a disservice if they don't. They will know *who* to introduce to you, as well. Wouldn't that be great—if your clients knew exactly who was a good fit for you, based on your areas of expertise? With this process you won't fear offending a client or feel obligated to take on as a client a referral who you feel isn't a good fit. And finally, you will be able to show your clients *how* to actually make an introduction by following a process you give them.

THE ADVOCATE REFERRAL PROCESS

Below is a generic variation of our Advocate Process, which we have helped literally hundreds of people customize to suit their own style and needs. There is a slight adjustment you need to make when presenting this process to a new client versus an existing client, because new clients have no expectations or frame of reference for how you conduct yourself with respect to referrals. It is, therefore, a good idea to practice and refine this approach with new people before you start presenting it to existing relationships.

With that in mind, at the signing ceremony when you bring on a new client, you can introduce the concept by pointing back to the initial meeting you had where you planted the seed. Remind them of what you said regarding The Uniqueness of My Approach bullet on the agenda by saying something like this:

> Mr. Client, you'll remember that at our first meeting I mentioned to you that invariably over the lifetime of our relationship there is a chance that a friend or family member will ask you about me or you may feel compelled to make an introduction. Now please understand, I'm not asking you to think of anyone right now. This is simply for down the road.

By introducing the concept that way, you are hypothetically suggesting that it might happen but not tying it to any expectation. Furthermore, you are not putting them on the spot. Contrast this approach to the way most people talk about referrals. Some people say, "I'm trying to grow my business. Could you give me the names and phone numbers of a few friends who you feel would benefit from my service (so that I can call them later today and make them non-friends—here are the white pages)?" That is just a tad needy, not to mention the optics aren't too good, don't you think?

Our approach is not a tactic or a form of psychological trickery, but the ironic twist to this is that by saying, "I'm not asking you to think of anyone right now…" you will actually prompt the client to present a name more frequently than if you say, "Can you think of anyone who might need my service? If so, could you give me their name and number?" Incidentally, if the client interrupts you and says that he or she in fact does want to introduce someone to you, just say:

> I appreciate it. Perhaps hold the thought for a moment
> and let me outline my process and then we can come back
> to that.

Continue with:

> Mr. Client, it is important that I explain "why" I have
> made the commitment to offer value-added services like
> this, "who" is a good fit for my services and then, of course,
> "how" to get the wheels in motion should a situation
> present itself.

By doing this, you are planting the seed that this is a service and introducing the concept of why, who and how.

> I provide a variety of value-added services that my clients
> really find beneficial. One of those services includes making
> myself available to act as a sounding board for friends and
> family members of my clients who have questions about
> my type of service. Now please understand that anyone you
> introduce to me does not need to become a client to take
> advantage of this service. I will make myself available to
> offer objective second opinions that your friend can then use
> to make informed decisions in the future (this is your *why*).

This is a powerful component because it tells your client that you aren't being needy nor will you try to sell to his friend. It also enables you to explain your sense of purpose and the personal fulfillment that comes from helping people make good decisions—whether or not they are clients!

> What is interesting is that on occasion I will meet a friend of a client this way and we really hit it off and decide to work together. Let me tell you *who* those people typically are.

At this point, you simply use your Triple-A Ideal Client Profile as a tool to take the abstracts of who is a good fit down to something tangible and memorable for your clients. They can conceptualize this instantly. Write "Triple-A" on the client's agenda and break down each point. Explain that you like working with people who take action in areas that are directly suited to your areas of expertise. Describe attitude and advocacy as important elements that you are unwavering on.

> I must also say that there are occasions where a client will introduce someone to me who presses me to become my client. However, if I don't feel there would be a good fit based on my Triple-A profile, I won't bring them on as a client and I hope you'll understand. I will, however, introduce them to someone who is a more suitable fit.

By projecting scarcity, you create a cachet in working with you and you give yourself an out if, in fact, you really don't wish to work with someone they refer.

> As I've mentioned before, I prefer to think of myself as a specialist rather than a generalist. My goal isn't to see how big I can get; it's to see how small I can stay. I know my capacity to serve, and if I go beyond my capacity by trying to

be all things to all people, the level of service we provide will get diluted and that will never do. This is why I prefer to be all things to some people and why I stick to that Triple-A profile.

This is a powerful validation for your clients that they are working with a professional who takes their business very seriously. You are making yourself very referable to the right kind of people with this approach.

Now, there is a process in place that my clients use for making introductions. If you find yourself in a situation where a friend asks you about me or you feel compelled to recommend me to someone, call me and get the wheels in motion. Tell me about your friend and give me their contact information and we'll take it from there. And of course, hold me accountable that anyone you introduce to me will receive the same level of professionalism and confidentiality that you receive. (This is **how** clients make an introduction.)

TRAIN YOUR CLIENTS TO REACH OUT TO YOU

At this point, most people say, "If you find yourself in a situation where you want to make an introduction or somebody asks you about me, give them my card and have them call me." When some entrepreneurs bring on a new client, they hand them a stack of business cards (with the bizarre hope that the client will carry the cards around with them everywhere they go) without realizing that the thickness of the stack of cards has a direct impact on the perception of neediness. (Here Mr. Client, keep a box of my cards handy.)

Additionally, you don't know when one of your Triple-A clients is going to talk about you and/or your services. It will happen. Next month, a year from now, who knows when, though? But you want your clients to be ready when it does happen.

Now, if your client is talking to a friend and your name or service comes up, your client may say to his friend, "Well, here, call my guy. Here's his phone number. Call him." As easy as it is for his friend to call you, it's easier not to because there's no relationship.

Worse than that, though, is that the Law of Diminishing Intent kicks in. Every day that goes by that he doesn't call you, the likelihood that he ever will fades greatly. Train your clients to come to the rescue. With a little guidance, you can transform your clients into power brokering advocates.

Let us give you a simple analogy. If we went to a party with you and we knew all fifty people there but you didn't know anyone, what would be easier for you—if we were to tell you to have fun and mingle, or if we walked around with you, introducing you to people? If you train your clients to tell their friends to call you every time you come up in a conversation, for every ten times that happens, you'll get one call. However, if you train your clients to call on behalf of their friends, nine out of ten times you'll get calls. Your clients already have a relationship with you and are predisposed to advocacy.

As we'll show you in a moment, with existing clients, you need to present this with a slight modification because to them this is new. On our website, there is a sample introductory template called the Code of Conduct Letter that you can send to your favorite clients to plant the seed with them. Or if you choose, the following is an introductory script you can use in an upcoming meeting with an existing client. It can be seamlessly integrated with the bulk of the scripting we just provided you above.

> Mr. Existing Client, I have come to the realization that
> there are a number of value-added services I provide that

many of my clients aren't aware of. I made this realization because recently I asked a number of my clients this simple question: When you talk about me to a friend, how do you describe me? Their answers were all over the map. With that in mind, I thought I would quickly explain that one of the value-added services I provide is that I will make myself available to act as a sounding board for friends and family members of my clients.

You would then go into the rest of the process we described earlier. When you combine this with the service matrix, Triple-A client profiling, the four Cs, organization and structure, as well as a Procedures Manual, you have made yourself extremely referable.

If you take the high road and if you are understated, referrals can really be positioned as a service. You are essentially explaining the fulfillment that comes from helping people make informed decisions. Successful decision-making is a matter of choice, not chance. Your sense of purpose in terms of *why* you are in business is tied to helping people make informed decisions, whether or not these people are, or ever become, clients. If you can convey that, you will attract a steady stream of quality endorsements.

Referral Checklist

✓ **Ensure your phraseology is attractive.**
   Many business owners tend to overuse the word referral in their client communications. While the word is not inherently bad, we believe it tends to make one appear needy, speaking more about how you benefit, rather than how the client benefits. We urge you to replace the word with the words introduce and recommend when you communicate the referral concept to your clients. This speaks more to an activity than it does to your productivity.

✓ **Standardize the Referral Process.**
Our experience shows it is not uncommon for a business owner's clients to feel a little handcuffed when talking about the business provider—you—in an intelligent fashion. Help them sound more compelling or they will develop their own phraseology (and you might not like what they choose to say). Tell them exactly how to refer to you and make this a dedicated part of your business. This is why the Triple-A concept is so helpful.

It might sound foreign or make you uncomfortable at first, but it's crucial to script your recommendation message, rehearse it, and then teach your clients to relay it when an opportune moment arises. A wishy-washy approach leads to wishy-washy results. You may get referrals from a casual approach, but if you want predictable results, use a consistent and dedicated approach.

Capture and chronicle your approaches. Show your team how it's done and have them follow suit. With easy-to-follow, predictable procedures come predictable successes.

✓ **Launch the Code of Conduct Letter to existing clients.**
If you are reluctant to introduce your new-and-improved Advocate Process on existing clients in person, you can send out a personalized version of the letter below to open the door in a low-key manner. This simple letter can be mailed by itself or included within a newsletter, sent with an invoice, or used as a dedicated piece in your review or update kit. In a nutshell, it describes for your client what occurs when you meet with the person your client recommends. This approach facilitates the recommendation process for your clients, helping them to conceptualize it and relay it to their friends. It also builds your clients' confidence and as a result they know you take this issue seriously and you'll make them look good when they recommend you.

Dear Mr. Client,

As you know, one of the most fulfilling aspects of my job is
helping people make informed decisions about their business needs. The puzzle has many pieces, and I truly enjoy
helping people put those pieces together. In this way, I can
help my clients face the future with anticipation, not
apprehension, and this is especially important during
times of economic uncertainty.

What's more, one of my biggest responsibilities is to help
people referred to me by my clients. When someone
endorses me to a friend or family member, they are putting
their name on the line, and I don't take that lightly. I owe it
to my clients to do a good job.

So if you feel compelled to introduce me to a friend, give
me a call and get the wheels in motion. Your friend does
not need to become a client to gain access to me and I will
act as a sounding board to help him or her make informed
decisions in the future.

✓ **Imprint everywhere.**
   Once you've introduced your Referral Process to your clients,
   you can't expect that they will remember it over the lifetime of
   your relationship. You'll have to keep reminding them. Trigger
   that moment of familiarity and recognition every chance you
   get. And here's what's great. In virtually every form of communication you have with your clients you can be reminding
   them subtly and professionally about the concept of referrals.
   You can do this in phone calls, newsletters, review meetings,
   letters, every form of communication.

Every time you talk to clients you have the chance to remind them about the concept of referrals in a very high-road manner. Take the call rotation as an example. Your client has been with you for six months. He's in your call rotation. In your conversation you ask him, "Hey, how's it going?" What you're looking for in this conversation is an opportunity for him to open the door so you can say something else. You ask, "How's business?" He says, "Fantastic. How's yours?" The door is open for you to respond by saying, "It's funny you should ask because recently a couple of my clients have introduced a friend or family member who's been interested in what we do or simply looking for the reassurance of a second opinion. You remember the process if that happens, right? Just give us a call. I don't want to claim miracles, but I'll either validate that the track they're on is right, or reveal a few minor adjustments they could make. Minor adjustments could lead to major improvements down the road, but either way, if they're a friend of yours, I'll make the time to answer their questions. And of course they don't need to become a client. I'll simply make myself available."

P.S.—Letters to Clients Are Great as Referral Reminders

The P.S. at the bottom of your letter is the most vividly read part of your correspondence and is a great place to put a call to action for referrals. As you know, a call to action is simply when you tell someone what you want them to do.

We love calls to action. A shampoo company increased their sales by thirty percent with one call to action. They put the call to action on the directions of the shampoo. (It's weird they need directions on how to use shampoo!) What was their call to action? The directions said, "put in, rinse out" or words to that effect. What was the call to action? "Repeat." Sales went up thirty percent—consumption went up thirty percent. Next time you get a referral from a client, just say to them, repeat. (Just kidding.)

The following is a sample postscript message:

> P.S. Now would be a great time to thank my clients for recommending me to their friends and family throughout the year. As you know, my business has been built on word-of-mouth advertising, and I take it as a tremendous compliment that you have the confidence in me to wave my flag. It really means a lot. I treat it as a huge responsibility and one that I never take lightly. Thanks.

You're not asking for a referral; you're simply reminding clients about the concept.

Again, it comes down to what is called stage-of-readiness. You don't know when a client will have the opportunity to talk about you to someone within their inner circle, but the opportunity will present itself. You want your client to be ready to persuasively describe you and then act as the bridge.

It bears repeating: What are your clients saying now to their friends when the moment of truth occurs? More important, what do you want your client to do? Do you want them to give their friends your number with a simple "You gotta call my guy, he's great"? Or would you prefer they ask if they should call on their friend's behalf? Your clients should be saying, "As a value-added service, my guy makes himself available to act as a sounding board for friends and family members of his clients. And you don't even need to become a client. I can call him to get the wheels in motion." Creating a steady stream of inbound calls from your clients calling on their friends' behalf will happen by choice, not by chance. It is by design. We don't mean to oversimplify things, but it is time-tested. The purity of it from the standpoint of service is that it is fulfilling; it feels right—for you and for your clients.

FRAME YOUR WAY TO SUCCESS

This concept, although simple, has repeatedly proven to be an effective reminder for clients. Frame the following quote in a simple eight-by-ten-inch frame and hang it on the wall in your office. And/ or put it on the back of your business card.

> An introduction to a friend by a client is a huge responsibility and a tremendous compliment that should never be taken lightly.
>
> Anonymous

If we had had a nickel for every time one of our clients told us of clients who, upon seeing the framed quote, said, "I didn't know you were accepting new referrals" or "I thought you were too busy to accept new clients" or "It never occurred to me to refer a friend to you," well, we'd be writing this book from a villa in Tuscany.

Before we move on, here's another gentle reminder about implementation. We encounter an extraordinary number of business owners who enroll in our Coaching and Consulting program who are—unbeknownst to them—on the verge of a breakthrough in their business. Typically, over the course of their careers, business owners experience dramatic growth in terms of expertise and sophistication. However, the systems in the business do not get developed at the same rate. The resulting disparity can be frustrating. The business owner hears about terrific activities like the Client Advisory Council, and the Advocate Process, yet few things get fully implemented or have any real staying power. No matter how cognizant they are of a great idea, they simply do not have the infrastructure to implement it and translate it into results over the long haul. Referrals are the lifeblood of your business, so here is a quick summary checklist to inspire you to implement the Advocate Process, if nothing else:

- ✓ Clients know what they can expect from me when I meet a friend of theirs.
- ✓ They know my Ideal Client Profile.
- ✓ They have a clear representation of my approach to service and can tell others about it.
- ✓ I keep them informed and up-to-date regularly and consistently.
- ✓ They know the processes and steps of how to introduce someone to my services.
- ✓ They know how I am paid.
- ✓ They are familiar with my team, and the responsibilities of each individual.

If you can't check all these items off, why not? If you could, wouldn't it be easier for your clients to refer you to others? In our experience, the answer is a resounding *yes*!

And we've seen countless examples of this in a number of different scenarios firsthand. We can recall how one client called us to explain that one his best clients had called, a day after being introduced to our client's why/who/how Referral Process, to invite him to a charitable function that he was attending. This is a client who was quite substantial yet had never referred anyone to our client. He then said that his client wanted to introduce a close friend to him at the function.

Our client called us to ask for our advice on how he could present his "elevator speech" to his client's friend when he was introduced to his client's friend and the inevitable question—"So, tell me what you do"—comes up.

As you might know, elevator speeches are quick little data dumps that people use to quickly explain to someone what it is you do. And they are inherently flawed because they are essentially "drive-by" sales pitches.

We told our client to not even "go there" with his elevator speech. We told him to use a variation of the why/who/how process in a low-key and attractive way while projecting scarcity and professionalism.

Sure enough, the friend asked him for his opinion on a timely issue and our client responded with this:

> You know, this probably isn't the best time to get into this. Why don't we just enjoy the moment here and let's set up a time to meet to discuss your question and any others in detail. As Mike [his client who made the introduction] probably told you, I make myself available to act as a sounding board for friends and family members of my clients. You don't need to become a client to take advantage of this service; however, people have told me that this process has been a great investment of their time. I have your card and I'll have my assistant contact you to set up a time that works for both of us. Sound fair?

They met and today they are working together.

Remember

» You don't need to ask for referrals. Position referrals as a service to your clients rather than as a favor to you and then remind your clients that you accept referrals throughout the lifetime of your relationship.

Take Action Now! (Weeks 8 & 9)

» Customize and then gain mastery of the Advocate Process templates found on our website, **www.paretoplatform.com**, and begin introducing the process to your clients.

» Visit **www.breakthroughbusinessdevelopment.com** to see updates and insights from the field on this topic and others.

CHAPTER 11
RECIPROCATE

If you want people to buy into your goals and
dreams, start by buying into theirs.

Duncan MacPherson and David Miller

The R in DART stands for *reciprocity*. This is a crucial part of
your activity plan because if you think about the Law of
Reciprocity, giving really starts the receiving process.

CREATE PROMOTIONAL PARTNERSHIPS
AND STRATEGIC ALLIANCES

If you look back on the concept of building pillars to create multiple
income streams, once you have your client pillar chugging along,
your second pillar should be that of promotional partners. These
are other like-minded professionals in your marketplace who are

interested in collaborating with someone like you. When you think of the concept of MVPs, the clients of these partners are some of your most predisposed prospects.

The key with promotional partnering, however, is that the concept has to be, as is consistent with our entire philosophy, positioned as a service, and ideally you need to be the driving force in such relationships. Many entrepreneurs attempt to engage in various forms of collaboration and the process unravels because they telegraph their motivation as simply a money grab or they passively sit and wait for others to push things forward. Yes, your approach must be forthright and transparent, but the philosophy behind it also must be clear. After all, you are trying to simplify people's lives and deliver value-added services that they'll actually value. Furthermore, you have to be the one who is continually breathing life into the concept. You can't be at the mercy of external dependencies. You have to be the one continually stirring the proverbial pot.

We've been exposed to countless examples of promotional partnering from a variety of sectors in the marketplace. We've seen accountants collaborate with lawyers and financial advisors for estate planning luncheons. We've seen home renovation firms collaborate with professional landscape architects. We've seen mortgage brokers align themselves with other lenders, like leasing specialists. We've seen business owners from a variety of walks of life create professional business networks consisting of a variety of business providers, to offer clients a turnkey array of trusted and accountable vendors.

We were in Tampa, Florida a while back for a conference and took a cab from the airport to the hotel convention center. The cab driver was a nice guy and asked where we were from. We told him Canada. And we all started talking about hockey. Big surprise. We had a great chat. (He didn't know where Calgary or Kelowna was, but he laughed hysterically when we told him that Calgary was so flat you could watch your dog run away for three days.)

Anyway, when he asked what kind of work we did, we told him we were marketing and business consultants. He said, "I love marketing. Want to hear a great story?" He started to tell us about this restaurant in Tampa called Bern's Steak House. We'd never been there, but apparently it's legendary. "Here's what's cool about Bern's. They're really good. But," he said, "as a cab driver, if I drop somebody off at Bern's for dinner, after I drop them off, I get to drive around back and get a free steak." That's pretty cool. Think about it. Somebody gets into his cab, or any cab, and says, "I'm hungry, take me somewhere," where are they going? I can just see him salivating. "Oh. We've gotta go to Bern's. I mean, *you've* gotta go to Bern's." This guy is an influencer. The cab driver said that the restaurant is so good, they could survive just on word of mouth from their clients, but they thrive because of the endorsements from these very powerful influencers.

A Great and Supportive CAST

You, too, could be a powerbroker and create a community of strategic alliances, but where do you start? Well, as usual, a great jumping-off point would be to look at your favorite clients. Who among your current clients are in business for themselves and would be receptive to a reciprocal business development process? We have an acronym (big surprise)—CAST, which stands for Client Advisory Support Team.

We arrived at the acronym CAST in an attempt to add some personality to the concept and make it memorable. If you really get into the spirit of the concept you'll see that it can unfold like the production of a stage play.

In our analogy, clients are the *audience*. The business system— your duplicable interaction with clients—serves as the *script* and is a well-thought-out plan of action written for their critical eye. The person making the recommendations and planning for the best possible outcome in the business provider-client relationship is you, the *director*. Finally, the business professionals who help to implement the plan are the *actors*, or players, if you will.

Think of your best client. Who is his director with respect to the range of complementary services and products he needs? In keeping with our stage play analogy, as the director of a production you should be in direct contact with the actors—the various service providers—to actively implement the script.

The greatest threat to a director occurs when he or she loses control or leaves the players to their own devices.

How does this happen? It would be easy to say clients allow this to happen because they don't have a relationship with their director based on an inherent level of trust. The opposite is also true. Directors allow this to happen because they haven't made the effort to build trust-based relationships with their clients. It's that simple.

> **Q:** How do other directors make contact with another director's client?
>
> **A:** Well, affluent people talk to other affluent people. *Source One* for this type of contact is the personal recommendation of a family member or friend. *Source Two* is, more important, the professional recommendation.

Let's say, in this scenario, that an accountant is recommending a financial advisor to his client. The client is very open to this type of professional recommendation because of the existing trust-based relationship with the professional making the recommendation.

However, as the director of the financial script, if you're the financial advisor, this type of incident is less likely to occur because you are integral in implementing the plan. You become the common factor linking the financial professionals involved in implementing a financial plan with the client.

Q: Should I recommend other business providers to a client? Why would I want to go to that trouble?

A: Yes, you should. It is easier than you think to recommend clients to CAST members you know and trust. After all, you should be developing open lines of communication with a client regarding all matters pertinent to their business. Recommending professionals who do excellent and necessary work is your responsibility, particularly if you're interested in your client's business remaining not only afloat, but also viable and ultimately successful.

The positive results are threefold. First, the client is more likely to remain loyal to you as a source of good information, thus reducing the chances they will be recommended away from you. Second, you secure your position as the primary relationship. Last but not least, creating a solid, reliable and trustworthy CAST will benefit the client immensely and will encourage the client to recommend other affluent people who seek this type of comprehensive service.

Keep in mind these basic and important facts about affluent clients:

1. Affluent clients have many different needs and use a wide array of solutions. Do you know who their providers are? They should be recommended and directed by you and/or be aware of your relationship with the client.

2. In the majority of cases, a client is recommended to a CAST member by a friend, family member, associate or another member of the client's CAST. You should make every effort to be the person directing the recommendations. That empowerment and accountability makes you even more trusted and

indispensable. Your relationship with the client should be the primary relationship within the CAST network.

3. Usually, a client's CAST members work in isolation. This is an opportunity for a proactive director to take the leading role in the CAST by integrating the members of the CAST and ensuring that all are reading the same script.

4. Each member of the CAST has a unique ability that adds strength to the overall production.

5. Like the director, other CAST members encourage and welcome recommendations and introductions to prospective clients.

6. In most cases, still with the financial services example, clients will already have a lawyer, accountant, tax preparer, banker or insurance agent they are using or have used in the past. However, it does not necessarily follow that they are satisfied with the services provided by these professionals. Do not make assumptions. Instead, ask the important questions. You may be surprised by the answers.

LAUNCHING THE CAST INITIATIVE

An effective CAST campaign may be implemented through the following steps.

Step 1

Begin developing a group of professionals for your best clients. You need look no further than your best clients. Either they themselves can play a role in the process, if they are in business for themselves, or they can introduce you to someone they trust. Poll each client for the members of *their* Client Advisory Support Team. You are, in essence, building a community and network of like-minded, non-competitive business professionals who need each other's services. (You could conduct a CAST Advisory Council to support this as it gathers momentum.) Every name represents the potential for a professional relationship. Contact each of these professionals and arrange an introductory meeting with the purpose of mutual awareness about the client you have in common. If, during this meeting, you are impressed by the services offered, consider recommending the person as a member of the CAST you offer to your other clients. Like you, all CAST professionals prefer to work by recommendation and they will welcome the opportunity to play a role in your business.

Incidentally, your Full Disclosure document can be modified to include a Professional Introductions section where you can speak to clients about your role as a power broker. Again, the CAST process, like all of your other initiatives, has to be presented (and perceived) as a service you are providing, rather than as a selling attempt. This has proven to be an effective way to help everyone conceptualize the process and help all involved see the benefits.

An important note: Confidentiality is a major component to building trusting relationships and to that end you must explain the parameters of your professional compliance to privacy.

Step 2

The second step is to find a CAST member with whom your client is unhappy. This is a golden opportunity to replace this person with a member from your CAST. By doing this, you are consolidating your position in the primary relationship.

Step 3

The third step is to build high-trust relationships with existing and potential CAST members. Most business owners have experienced the situation where they've provided multiple referrals to an accountant or lawyer, for instance, only to be forgotten at subsequent client meetings. Such situations occur because referrals are not sufficient incentives for people to reciprocate. A referral is really only a type of lead.

A recommendation, on the other hand, is very different. It assumes a transfer of trust from one professional to another. As we've mentioned on several occasions, the most crucial elements of a professional career are trust and integrity. Most professionals will not risk losing these elements with a client by making light of a recommendation made to another professional. In other words, you must develop a high degree of trust with CAST members.

In order to build high levels of trust, you must demonstrate consistency, congruency, credibility and, above all, integrity and accountability. The rule of relationship building is to be patient, as it will take time, and to have frequent contact based on genuine intent.

In the beginning stages of a professional relationship, merely referring business will not build the level of trust you need in order to create a successful CAST. Referring business is a given.

Beyond that, you must construct a deliberate, meaningful service package for your CAST members and potential CAST members, one that you deliver consistently. In this way, a CAST member is much like a client. Some examples you may wish to use in your CAST package are quarterly phone calls, articles of interest, invitations to select client events, copies of your newsletter and annual anchors (such as Thanksgiving/birthday cards).

Once you have decided on your approach, enter it into your contact management system to ensure consistency. As recommendations start to come back to you, send acknowledgments for the trust and confidence, not for the business. Say thank you for the continued trust and confidence instead of thank you for the business.

IT IS WORTH THE EFFORT

Creating, directing and supporting a CAST is not an easy task. It is similar to developing a solid base of affluent clients through the process of building client confidence and encouraging client recommendations. You may ask yourself, "Is this degree of effort going to be worth it? I have spent considerable time and effort building my client base. Why bother with a CAST when I can enjoy the benefits of my existing client base?" Unless you are completely confident you are indispensable and irreplaceable to each and every affluent client, you need to secure the relationship you have with your clients. Being the director of a trusted, competent CAST will build a virtual wall around your clients. The value of your relationship with your clients will increase exponentially as you secure your position as the director of their business provisions.

That said, you may be feeling that this is a decent idea but you don't yet have the time to commit to it fully. There is a simple way to launch the concept to get the wheels in motion. Make a listing of all of your existing business relationships—not in terms of actual names but sectors of the marketplace. List the various services in which you have a meaningful contact onto a plastic bookmark and send it to your clients with a letter that says:

> As you know, I'm very well connected in the business community. Clients call me regularly to ask if I have a contact in a given sector and if I could introduce them to one of my contacts. Here is a listing of the various sectors in the marketplace in which I have a very good relationship. Just slide this into your yellow pages and if ever you need any

of these (e.g., accountant, computer guru) call me and I'll make an introduction.

It is an easy way to position yourself as a power broker. Your clients will make you the "go-to" person to contact before they buy anything. You may have a client call and say, "Well, I want to buy a new car. Should I buy or lease?" Even if you're not even remotely connected to the car business, you can say, "Let me make a call for you." Look out for people and they will look out for you. The Law of Reciprocity is powerful.

As a caveat, be sure to explain the rules of engagement to anybody you recommend. Simply say,

> Look. If I ever introduce somebody to you, the world stops. Drop everything and absolutely shower this person with goodwill and service. And I'll do the same for everyone you introduce to me.

In the business development world, this mindset is referred to Reciprocal Endorsed Marketing, or **REM** for short. It speaks to a commitment that a group of professionals have for each other, both in terms of endorsement support and plain old patronage. This reminds us of a classic example. David Ogilvy, easily our favorite marketing guru ever, lived and breathed this approach. When his advertising firm was awarded the contract for Rolls Royce, he immediately went out and bought one of their cars. He made a commitment that spoke volumes. Make a commitment to your partners and they will commit to you.

Before we shift gears, we'll say it again: Your best prospective clients are the friends and family members of your existing clients. They are number one. Your second best are existing customers, who could become clients. A close third on the MVP list are the clients of promotional partners.

Remember

» Be a power broker. Giving really does start the receiving process.

Take Action Now! (Week 10)

» Review the CAST scripting and process found on our website, **www.paretoplatform.com**.

» Visit **www.breakthroughbusinessdevelopment.com** to see updates and insights from the field on this topic and others.

CHAPTER 12
THANK

Not saying thanks when a client brings value to you would be like not feeding the goose that lays the golden eggs.

Marketing Maxim

The T in DART is for *thanks*. New clients, existing clients, promotional partners, vendors and staff bring value to you every day. A major part of your code of conduct must include activities that pay tribute to that value. In a perfect world, these moments of truth would never go unrecognized.

WHEN SOMEONE BECOMES A NEW CLIENT

It is a big deal when new clients empower you to provide products or services, especially if they have left another business provider. Remember, it's all about contrast. Once they move over to you, they are going to compare the two of you. Furthermore, if that client has been referred to you by a client or strategic alliance, those two people—the referrer and the new client—are eventually going to meet and talk about you.

What do you do to ensure the new client not only makes favorable comparisons in his own mind, but also goes back to the source of the referral and describes how he was dazzled? Your efforts will go a long way towards prompting your new client to say, "You were right. She really is great!" That validation for an existing client can be the tipping point to a continuous stream of recommendations in the future.

At the very least, you must send a personalized thank you card to a new client immediately after they have come on board with you. Mere moments after the proverbial signing ceremony, send a nice card that will have impact and shelf life. Please be careful with the phraseology. Do not write "Thanks for the business." This only recognizes the benefits to you (and it conjures up an image of your running around the office getting high fives). Make the message about them. Write something that demonstrates to the client that you were really paying attention. Make reference to something they revealed to you about themselves. Speak to the activity and the chemistry that you have already developed.

For example:

> I really enjoyed meeting with you today. It was fun listening
> to you describe your new boat. I'm looking forward to a great
> relationship. Welcome aboard!

The bottom line is for you to be understated yet radiate an attractive impression. You don't actually need the business. (You'll take it, but you don't need it, right?!?) By conveying to new clients that your utmost fulfillment comes from meeting and working with great people, you make a powerful statement about your commitment to helping people achieve their goals.

Ultimately, the thank you card is just the start. We encourage our clients to use a four- or five-step advocate process following the card. These other steps in the process, implemented during the first thirty to forty-five days of the new relationship, are designed to counter any buyer's remorse and further validate the client's decision to select you, while fast-tracking him or her to advocate status.

THE FIVE-STEP NEW CLIENT WELCOME PROCESS

In order to convert new clients to advocate status as quickly as possible, take a good look at your current New Client Welcome Process. Although this is just one small component, it's one you can easily implement. We recommend this five-step process (or something similar) for two simple reasons. First, your new client will inevitably give important feedback to the person who introduced the two of you (if, in fact, they came to you by way of introduction), and second, a new client who has been referred is predisposed to referring someone else as well. You are at your highest level of refer-ability with these people early in the relationship. They have—themselves—just been through the process and were (ideally) dazzled. They are better qualified than anyone else to refer you. This is especially true at the beginning of your relationship when their enthusiasm for you is fresh. People like to brag. It's called The Law of Approval. Many people like to brag about their own decisions to gain the approval of others and thus further validate their great decision. Give them something to brag about.

Here is a simplified version of the New Client Welcome Process that you can implement with minimal expense. You'll want to customize this for your own unique situation, but this baseline will get you started:

Step 1

Start archiving FORM (Family, Occupation, Recreation, Message) information on the client and family from the beginning of your relationship with every client. Ideally you will be subtle as you and your team start compiling the information that gets revealed as the relationship unfolds. You can accelerate the process by actually giving the new client a FORM questionnaire once they come on board. If a client ever asks why you need non-business-specific information, use the following to help explain your intentions in a positive way: "It is one of my top goals to bring my clients exceptional value, and it helps me to do a better job if I know what it is they value."

Step 2

As mentioned, be sure to send a nice card after the initial meeting to continue the chemistry-building process. Personalize your greeting and write it by hand. Try to include something the client revealed about his or her situation or interests.

Step 3

Approximately one week after the new client has come on board, send a formal welcome letter informing the client of your appreciation at being selected. Also mention that you and your team understand the scope of responsibility involved. Introduce the members of your team, including their job descriptions and telephone numbers. Add a P.S. to remind your new client that you and your team are always available to answer questions for friends and family members, too.

Step 4

Approximately two weeks after the new client has come on board, send a good-quality welcome binder complete with divider tabs and a letter. In the letter, explain your realization of the vast quantities of information they will receive from you (statements, newsletters, updates, etc.) and your pride in helping people keep it organized. The tabs could be labeled according to the services you provide. Also be sure to include your Full Disclosure document—AKA a complete listing of your services as well as your CAST concept. (Hopefully you will have introduced this information during the signing ceremony, but this will reinforce it.) They will refer back as their needs change in the future.

You may be tempted to give the binder to your new client upon the signing, but instead, show it to them, tell them you will get it set up and then send it out. Its arrival will be well-received.

NOTE: You can provide the binder to current Triple-A clients at a future review meeting. Simply explain how you are enhancing client service and that the binder is part of that new approach. Walk them through it—especially your full listing of services, as well as CAST—and watch how your clients respond. It's a simple concept that often creates dramatic results.

Step 5

When your new client receives their first statement or invoice from your firm, have a team member call to walk them through it and answer any questions or concerns they may have. This refreshingly courteous call is part of the contrast-building process designed to demonstrate your code of conduct. If you follow this process, your new clients will feel as though they have received more value from you in the first few days than they did from their former provider in an entire year. As a result, you will be that much more referable.

SAYING THANKS FOR A REFERRAL: FEED THE GOOSE

An endorsement is one of the biggest compliments—and responsibilities—you can ever receive. Show your clients you don't take the vote of confidence lightly. Again, pay tribute to the activity, not the productivity. Rather than sending a card saying, "Thanks for referring Bob to me," say instead, "Thanks for introducing Bob to me." Again, this slight adjustment in phraseology does not speak to your needs, but rather to theirs.

We'll say it again: You must never look needy. The marketplace rewards what we earn and deserve. A profound distinction exists between seeming demanding or needy and being deserving. When you take the latter—the high road—people will be easily convinced to work with you and will go to work convincing other people on your behalf. The point is, though, that as the referral floodgates begin to swing open, don't take them for granted by letting an *entitlement* mindset creep in. Say *thanks* in a meaningful way that has *both impact and shelf life* and the referrals will continue to flow.

We have countless examples of business owners who are close to hitting the mark but miss ever so slightly. A case in point is a friend we have in the leasing business. We sent him a huge referral. It made his year. He knows we play golf, so he sent a few sleeves of golf balls. We called him up, laughing, to say, "Hey, nice impact, lousy shelf life." The balls didn't last long; they got drilled into forests and ponds the very next round we played. We told him he should have sent us a golf magazine loaded with golfing tips. That would have been about the same price but with much better shelf life. Every month for a year, when the magazine arrived, we'd be thinking about him.

Again, the best way to have impact is to apply FORM. We know one business owner whose client's son was a sports nut and loved hockey. After this particular client sent a meaty referral to our client, he responded by sending the father and son a pair of hockey tickets.

Pretty good, we thought, but our client didn't stop there. He also dug deep and sent the son an NHL jersey! That was certainly more enduring than just the tickets. Every time the son wears the jersey, what goes through his dad's mind?

GOOD BRANDING IS OUTSTANDING

An essential component that ties the Referral Process together with *saying thanks* to your clients is to create personal branding that people can identify with. Good branding personifies and differentiates you. Your brand is what makes you different, helps you stand out and enables your clients to easily see why and how you and your services are special. Your branding is a reflection of you and is in essence an extension of your Unique Value Proposition (UVP). When people think of Volvo, they instantly think of safety. When people think of Maui, they think of relaxation and a slower pace. Remember Miller Lite? Tastes great! Less filling!

What do people instantly think of when they think of you? What is their perception, and do they use that to help them describe you to others? If you have created a brand, your clients can easily wave your flag with meaningful specifics. Without these specifics, you run the danger of either being taken for granted or just swimming in a pool of sameness where, rather than being indispensable to your clients, you are interchangeable with your competitors. The following are a few examples.

Establish a Foundation

Cicero, in ancient Rome, said in essence, "Ask not what your community can do for you, ask what you can do for your community." We all know the modern version of that quote, but the spirit has a direct correlation to entrepreneurs. By that we mean, inject a community feel into your marketing efforts to say *thanks* for everything you get from it and also to help establish your personal brand.

Identify with a community event or charitable organization or create one of your own. Sponsor a rising sports star. Create a scholarship for kids that you will contribute to every time you bring on a new client or receive a referral. Not only does it contribute to your business success and brand identity, it also contributes to your personal fulfillment.

At Pareto Platform we began an Excess Capacity Campaign that was extremely well-received by our clients. Here's how it works. When we dramatically enhanced our servers and technology backbone, we created a lot of extra capacity in terms of how many subscribers we could effectively service. We decided to put that capacity to use. We offered our clients the opportunity to provide our platform free of charge to a charity that they themselves had a connection to. Fundraising organizations need to manage their relationships with donors, just as businesses need to with clients. This didn't really cost us much but our clients were tremendously appreciative. It adds to our branding and gives our clients something to brag about above and beyond the obvious.

Do you have an opportunity to offer excess capacity to a non-profit organization via a client? Can you provide pro bono service to someone who might not be able to afford it? As personal development guru Jim Rohn advised us, "In business, don't just focus on making a profit. Leave a profit, too. Make things better than you found them."

Milestone Recognition

On a frequent basis, meaningful events or milestones occur in your clients' lives. These are moments of truth that you could pay tribute to.

We have a financial advisor client who, in a conversation with *his* best client said, "So, what are you doing this weekend?" His best client answered, "Oh, we're going to my son's graduation, finally." The (now) proud (and relieved) dad continued with details of his long-time concerns the kid would never get through school because it took a long time with stops and starts, trips to Europe and so on. Apparently the kid had to *find himself*. Our client tells us about the conversation and our first response was, "That's soul baring. That's not something everybody would do and it says a lot about your relationship. This guy trusts you. What are you going to do? This moment of truth could take your relationship to another level altogether." Our client didn't have an answer, so we gave him one. "Go out and buy the book *The Richest Man in Babylon*."

Our client sent the book to the kid with a card congratulating him. (Again, remember the advice of Confucius: "Dig your well before you're thirsty." This could be a future client.) The card said, "Hey, congratulations. Way to go! This is the only book you'll need to ensure your financial future." The kid's father called back and said, "That was impressive. My kid read it in one sitting. If I had given it to him, he wouldn't have read it. It came from you and transformed the way he thinks about money. You should hear him."

Clearly, these examples are value-added in nature. We aren't suggesting that your branding shouldn't be connected to the quality of your skills and competencies. What we are suggesting is that if your brand can be tied to building chemistry it will complement your credentials. Apply the two along with consistency and congruency and your business will have no limits.

IMPROVING COMMUNICATION IS KEY

You already know this, but here's a gentle reminder. The single activity that has the greatest impact on your ability to competitor-proof your favorite clients and stimulate quality referrals is consistent communication. Proactively convey to a client that you genuinely value the relationship. This is without question the foundation of your daily marketing code of conduct. Clearly, the cornerstone of this message is the style and manner in which you demonstrate your sincere appreciation when the client brings value to you.

There are all kinds of moments-of-truth examples that you could be responding to. (We discussed a number of them back when we talked about FORM.) A client has a meaningful birthday or anniversary. Pay tribute to these things. They're important. Another client expands his business and moves to a new, larger facility. Have a professional photographer to take a picture of their new building. Get it framed. It won't cost a lot of money but the impact and shelf life are huge. Stop for a second to pay tribute when these moments of truth occur. Make an effort to stand out. Just as we suggested with Thanksgiving cards, stop and say thanks for a great relationship.

Remember

> » When someone brings value to you, it's a moment of truth that defines your relationship. Pay tribute in a way that has impact and shelf life.

Take Action Now! (Week 11)

> » Refer to the Milestone and Moment of Truth guidelines on our website, **www.paretoplatform.com**, and strive to make this process habitual.

> » Visit **www.breakthroughbusinessdevelopment.com** to see updates and insights from the field on this topic and others.

A FINAL WORD BEFORE WE SHIFT FROM CLIENT-CENTERED MARKETING TO PROSPECTING

As we pointed out earlier, the key to success is to make the implementation of DART-related activities *habitual*. The best way to achieve that is to create automated processes that you and your team can deploy effortlessly. They are the surefire way to create consistency in your business. As you know, your clients crave consistency because it is the foundation of trust in all levels of the business world. People use a drive-through at a fast-food restaurant repeatedly, not because of the quality of the food but because it saves time and they know what to expect. There are no surprises. They trust it. (Imagine how many burgers they would sell if the burgers were actually good?!) People stay loyal to a dentist because their expectations will at least be met, if not, exceeded. The moment the service falls below expectations, cracks in the loyalty foundation begin to appear.

At the risk of getting too technical, an automated process is defined as any repetitive activity involving a series of different steps. Customer service is an excellent example. Set up your database (even off-the-shelf contact management software will enable you to do this) to remind you of activities relative to clients' FORM information. Depending on the classification of each client, you and your team may have up to twenty-five activities or "touches" per year for a Triple-A client. By coding your clients in the database and then by designing your service matrix—that is, the specific activities for each client classification—the database will automatically notify you or the appropriate member of your team when any of these activities are to be completed. These activities can then be set up to renew on an annual basis for an indefinite period of time.

To identify a process as one worthy of automation, we look for an activity requiring multiple steps to be completed sequentially.

Therefore, anything in your business approach that meets this criterion can have an automated process designed for it. New Client Welcome, Anniversary or Milestone Recognition or anything else that comes to mind can be included. As always, your FORM information will prove to be invaluable.

Identify, recognize and define automated processes. It's important. Automated processes promote consistency and congruency, create a pathway to enhance chemistry and help create a memorable client experience. Clients learn your patterns and come to expect them. Once the expectations have been set, and met, your clients will communicate your patterns to others. When they do, people like themselves are naturally and easily recommended to you.

To create one automated process, you must create an architecture that can be converted to a digital format. The digital format is then housed on your database. As a result, you will not have to be concerned with the ensuing steps on a daily basis. The database informs each and every person in your organization exactly what is to be completed and when.

Four steps are involved in creating an automated process.

1. Name the process and provide a short description so others will understand the purpose.

2. Record each step of the process.

3. Define the specific elements of each step. The elements are *who, what, when* and *how*.

4. Store all this information in the database. The database will monitor activity as well as completion.

Once your automated processes are in place, you, your staff and your clients will notice a significant difference in how you interact.

SHAMELESS PLUG FOR THE PARETO PLATFORM

Clearly it was the concept of automated processes that inspired us to create the Pareto Platform, our own proprietary business development tool integrated with a flexible client relationship manager. If you aren't interested in reinventing the wheel, visit our website at **www.paretoplatform.com** and allow us to outline its functionality. This will enable you to determine if it is a fit for your business.

CHAPTER 13
PROSPECT TARGET MARKETING

O nce you have your client pillar predictably producing revenue, you can then extend to the promotional partnering pillar. If you are already reasonably efficient, those two pillars can be managed in duality. If, after deploying and refining the processes for the first two and you still find yourself with excess time capacity, then, and only then, can you consider the third pillar—prospect target marketing.

Don't misinterpret what we're saying here. Prospecting *can* be an integral part of your business development approach and mindset. Our concern, however—and this stems from witnessing countless examples firsthand—is that we don't want you to pursue prospect target marketing at the expense of lower-hanging fruit.

Let's come full circle back to the MVP concept. Your Most Valuable Prospects are as follows:

- friends and family members of existing clients based on the Rule of Fifty-Two
- customers who could become fully empowering clients based on the Loyalty Ladder
- clients of promotional partners based on CAST and the Law of Reciprocity
- target market prospects

Based on the above list, and unless you have a brand new business, be certain that you have the first three opportunities chugging along in a predictable and sustainable way before you engage in pure prospect target marketing.

Some would dispute this approach, saying that they don't have time to wait for their first two pillars to start bearing additional fruit. Prospecting can garner more immediate impact. If you are thinking that way, consider this: Many of our clients haven't engaged in pure prospecting in years. Zero. They have adopted the "attract rather than chase" philosophy and view every expenditure of effort with clients as an investment that will always pay the best return. It goes beyond just the obvious.

Yes, it is better to work those who are already convinced than it is to try to continually convince new people, but keep in mind that all business development efforts have trickle-down benefits. You continually insulate relationships from competitive factors, enhance trust for empowerment and refer-ability and drive the value of your business higher. Furthermore, existing client relationships factor heavily when placing a valuation on a business. It is for those reasons that client-focused marketing and promotional partnering are the ultimate in multitasking activities.

That said, if you are new to business and don't have a lot of existing clients yet or if your business is established and has the first two pillars humming along, you can then certainly consider these concepts sooner. Our note of caution is that you don't want to forget about how valuable your existing client relationships are as you set out to attract new ones.

ON TO PROSPECTING

Let's differentiate between advertising and prospect target marketing. We're not the biggest fans of classic advertising for small entrepreneurs for a variety of reasons. There is an old saying, "Half of all advertising is wasted. We just don't know which half." A lot of advertising is spray and pray. Throw stuff out there and hope for the best. Results of promotional efforts must be quantifiable. Don't engage in *hope* advertising, where you hope it's going to work. Just because your competitors are doing it or just because you have the budget doesn't mean it is appropriate for you.

Prospect target marketing is an entirely different conversation. It is far more precise and efficient. Advertising is broadcasting; target marketing is narrowcasting. It might not be as glamorous, but the return on investment is dramatically better.

AVOID SPRAY-AND-PRAY MARKETING

We know what we're talking about here, not just because of our work in our "laboratory"—our coaching and consulting clients—but also in our own business development efforts. Every now and again we get lured back into the black hole known as broadcasting. When we started promoting our Pareto Platform, we bought full-page ads, albeit in magazines that were targeted to our audience, that were classic spray-and-pray ads. The ads talked about the attributes of our Platform and created compelling reasons why readers should visit our website and take our introductory tour. In one case, we got faked out because a magazine had a circulation of eighty thousand readers. We thought, "how could we go wrong?" When the dust cleared, one hundred people went to our website and a couple took action. Not exactly stellar results.

Broadcast advertising like that is interruptive. You're flipping through a magazine, and come across our ad that interrupts what you're reading. You didn't buy the magazine for the ads; you bought it for the content. We're hoping you'll shift your focus from the article you were reading to our message and feel compelled to take action. Not a very predictable scenario.

Our point in mentioning this right up front is simple. We want you to scrutinize your current prospecting efforts and ask yourself if they have quantifiable impact or if they are broadcast "hope" marketing approaches.

There are so many different prospecting options. Contrast the interruptive magazine campaign we just described to our next effort. After we scolded each other for breaking one of our own etched-in-stone marketing rules, we then launched our search engine optimization and adwords campaign on Google. (There are a variety of good books available on the topic.)

This campaign was much more effective, first and foremost because we turned the tables. With the broadcasting campaign, we hoped people would stumble into our ad, stop what they were doing and visit our website. With the search engine campaign, people came looking for us. When people searched on Google for the trigger words we selected, our ads came up on the side of browser window. People who were predisposed clicked on them and instantly went to our website. In our initial test campaign, we spent eighteen hundred dollars and received in excess of nine hundred hits to our website, with surprising conversion. Keep in mind, these were people who were looking for what we sold; we weren't looking for them. Prospecting is like mining for gold. You have to sift a lot of dirt to find an ounce of gold, but you aren't trying to turn the dirt *into* gold. That is the difference between "finding" prospects and trying to "create" them.

Broadcasting is expensive, it's time-consuming, it's laborious and worst of all it sets you up for the most brutal emotion in marketing: *anticappointment!* You put it out there, you cross your fingers, anticipate, but are—in the end—disappointed. Trade shows, billboards, radio, newspaper ads, cold-calling and the like are broadcasting efforts that are often the least efficient yet most expensive ways to prospect. They can give a certain measure of instant gratification, but after that it's like a shooting star, fading quickly and forgotten. (We worked a trade show booth a long time ago that was a complete waste of time—on an hourly basis we earned less money than a parking meter would have.)

Narrowcasted marketing is the way to go. You zero in on specific, high-value, geographic, demographic, socioeconomic target markets and turn them upside down methodically over a period of time.

SPECIALIZE, DON'T GENERALIZE

The first point to consider on narrowcasting is this: Position yourself as a specialist. There are two types or marketers—specialists and generalists. As we've said before, generalists try to be all things to all people and promote horizontally. Specialists try to be all things to some people and promote vertically. In the process, specialists radiate more cachet and professionalism.

The key point of difference is that specialists realize that prospecting is a process, not a random, haphazard activity. The first step they take in the process once they've identified a target market is to develop an insider's reputation. This is achieved when the prospects within your target market identify you as being elite and head and shoulders above your competitors because of your awareness and focus for the sector. One of the best ways to achieve this is to identify an inside champion— ideally an existing client or simply an acquaintance in the sector you wish to expand your reach within—who can help you understand the target market better and in the process make you more attractive.

As usual, the best place to start is with your clients. Think about your existing Triple-A clients. What do they do? Where do they live? Choose one of them. We've seen countless examples of prospect target marketing pillars that were built on a foundation of one existing client relationship that over time developed into dozens and on occasion literally hundreds of relationships with similar clients.

We've seen a financial advisor build a practice consisting of over forty high-net-worth dentists that stemmed from the fact that his wife was a dental hygienist. She introduced her husband to a dentist, told him everything he ever wanted to know about dentistry and, well, the rest is history.

We know of an accountant who built a business consisting of clients who were MBA grads. As an MBA himself, he would look for announcements from universities showcasing their latest graduates and send congratulatory letters to them along with an invitation to meet to discuss any financial issues that might be on their minds.

To this day though, our favorite example of this business development approach was a client of ours—a very bright and successful financial advisor—who blew the lid off his business in an incredible fashion.

As we discussed this concept with him, he revealed that his number one client owned an engineering firm. We said, "Engineers. Let's target engineers." He said, "Nope. I don't want another engineer." (Apparently he had some issues with engineers!)

His second-best client was a dairy farmer (referred to him by his assistant's dad, who happened to be a dairy farmer). We asked, "How's your relationship with this guy?" "Uh, fantastic," he told us. We advised, "Take him out for lunch, pick his brain and basically ask him what you need to do to make yourself attractive to people just like him. Tell him, 'If I had my way, I'd have a hundred clients like you. You perfectly match my Ideal Client Profile, plus you are a lot of fun to talk to.'" Our client called us after that little lunch and said, "This is going to be amazing. We had a great meeting and he is definitely going to help me out."

We then told him to build on this momentum. "Develop an insider's reputation where other dairy farmers view you as a specialist. Learn everything you need to know about the sector." Do you know there is a magazine called *The Holstein Journal*? Everything you ever wanted to know about cows. There's enough interesting stuff about cows to fill a magazine every month. Not only did he read the magazine, he eventually had some of his articles published in it. You walk into his office today and you'll see pictures of his clients standing beside their big cows with ribbons on them. (Betsy—Top Milker Award!?! We're not sure what they win awards for.) He became the go-to guy for dairy farmers.

Instead of being all over the map, he narrowed his focus, became a specialist, increased his visibility, built a relationship with an inside champion and then developed an insider's reputation. This same scenario is easily adaptable to various geographic regions and marketplace sectors.

AN INSIDER'S REPUTATION MAKES YOU STAND OUT FROM THE PACK

Speaking of financial advisors, another client of ours established a unique niche. He's a financial advisor to airline pilots. He has done this so well that he can saunter up to a group of random airline pilots in an airport and intelligently participate in their conversation and can even use the lingo that comes only from associating with pilots on a very regular basis. This gift of the aeronautical gab is not accidental.

This advisor started his narrowcasting efforts with two of his clients who were pilots. It was purely chance and good fortune that he attracted the two in the first place. They didn't know each other and he knew virtually nothing about the typical life of a pilot. But once he realized that he had an untapped opportunity in the form of these potential inside champions, he invited both of them out to lunch and began the process of developing an insider's reputation. "I'm fascinated with what you do and I really like working with you. In a perfect world, I would like to deal extensively with people just like you. Would you please help me understand how to become more attractive to people in your line of work?"

He then asked his pilot clients the following questions:

- What is the life of a pilot like?
- What challenges do you face?
- What is important to you?
- What could make your life better?
- What publications could I read to better understand your industry?

This advisor now deals with many airline pilots. His reputation precedes him. He is the go-to guy for pilots. Anytime the subject of money comes up with one of his pilot clients and their inner circle, it is a knee-jerk reaction for his clients to say, "You have to talk to my advisor. He understands us."

The Law of Environment tells us people tend to congregate with other people who are pretty much like themselves. Doctors chum with other doctors, chiropractors with other chiropractors, and so forth.

If you decide to become a specialist for a particular sector, use the Law of Environment to your advantage. One of your clients will be at a gathering with others in your chosen demographic, and someone will probably raise the subject of business providers—your area of expertise—and express dissatisfaction with their current situation. Armed with the dedicated Advocate Process you have put in place, your client will make a compelling case for you.

Although some generalist business owners have done very well trying to be all things to all people, those who have built their business by offering focused services to a particular sector have a distinct and simple advantage: Their clients have a great story to tell. It's compelling to hear about someone who specializes in dealing with people who are just like you. Why would you want to go anywhere else? Best of all, your efforts in specializing compound. In time, your efforts take on a life of their own and then the pieces start to fall into place.

We've also seen this work in concert with promotional partnering efforts and target marketing. We've seen an accountant who specializes in working with business owners collaborate with business brokers— professionals who help people buy and sell businesses. We've seen a lawyer who creates estate plans for high-net-worth clients collaborate with high-caliber insurance specialists who provide a host of essential services to affluent families. We've seen a financial advisor who works with professional athletes collaborate with accountants who also specialize in working with professional athletes. In each of these and other scenarios, the breakthroughs have been staggering. The sky is the limit if you are focused, patient and diligent.

SO YOU'VE DECIDED TO SPECIALIZE…NOW WHAT?

It is crucial that you understand what is referred to in marketing as "the stage of readiness." When you identify your specific target markets and start marketing to them, resign yourself to the fact that you don't know when the prospects you're targeting will be ready to talk to you. It's just a matter of time, but it will take time. Again, from personal experience, we know that in your attempts to build contrast and predisposition, you have to build a degree of familiarity and comfort with a prospective client. Understanding this will remind you to be patient and save you some stress. Remember, stress in business stems from a lot of things, including unrealistic expectations. The gap between when you want something to happen and when it actually happens is often where stress is born.

Your prospecting efforts are designed to also counter the Law of Diminishing Intent. This immutable law simply reminds us that when people consider taking action on something, they had better act immediately. If they don't, their intent will diminish and fade. This occurs in marketing when a prospective client considers a prospecting offer. If they put it off, the likelihood they will act later diminishes. Keep in mind that they aren't necessarily saying no. They could be saying not now or I don't know, which is why you need to implement a campaign that follows the concepts below and patiently position yourself as the go-to provider when the prospective client is ready to act.

CONVERTING PROSPECTS TO CLIENTS WITH AICA

AICA is an acronym (naturally) that frames the concept of prospecting with these four tenets: *attention, interest, confidence* and *action.*

The First A in AICA Stands for *Attention*

Consider how many wireless signals are swirling around you right now. Hundreds, perhaps thousands. If you have the right receiver you can tune in any of them. If you don't, they continue to invisibly swirl around, unnoticed by you.

Your prospective clients are pounded with hundreds of marketing signals every day. If those signals don't get the person's attention, they won't be received. They will be ignored or dismissed. Your marketing efforts have to stand out and get their attention. Whether you're using a flyer, an ad in the yellow pages, email marketing, a search engine campaign or a direct mail letter, you need a hook to get the person's attention immediately. The headline at the top of your advertising ve-hicle must say something that speaks to the prospect and shakes him or her out of their fog. If you study marketing, you will find that most headlines make a promise statement of something positive or present a problem the prospect can relate to.

For purposes of illustration, we'll use direct mail as our example marketing medium. (We'll talk about other prospecting mechanisms towards the end of this section.) For what it's worth, we are big fans of extremely well-targeted "small-batch" direct mail campaigns. Many people would, in this era, dismiss direct mail as being obsolete. The concept itself is not flawed; however, nine out of ten campaigns are flawed because of mistakes made by the marketers.

People still like getting mail but most of us sort it over a garbage can. If the mail you send is not distinctive and doesn't get the recipient's attention, you might as well throw it in your own garbage can and save the stamps.

Believe it or not, a great way to get a recipient's instant attention is to use lumpy mail. A small-batch campaign with something lumpy like a fridge magnet will always outperform a larger campaign sent to more people but without the lumpy insert.

So, assuming the recipient opens your letter, you then need to encourage them to read it. As hinted, the opening headline must get their attention. Allow us to expand on the headline concept by integrating yet another acronym, PAS, within AICA. PAS stands for *problem, agitate, solve.* The best headline you can use in any letter (or any medium for that matter) presents a problem that the reader can relate to. Every time someone actually reads your marketing piece, they either connect with it and say "me too" or they dismiss it and say "so what." A problem is a perfect way to achieve the "me too" connection.

For example, a landscape architect sending a campaign to an affluent neighborhood could use the following headline:

"The Top Ten Mistakes Homeowners Make When Landscaping"

An accountant targeting business owners could use this headline:

"The Seven Most Common Tax Planning Mistakes and How to Avoid Them"

A dentist sending a campaign to an affluent neighborhood could use this:

"Have You Experienced Pain-Free Sedation Dentistry?"

An insurance broker could use this:

"Insurance Is Better to Have and Not Need than to Need and Not Have"

Our favorite headline was a campaign to restaurants from a restaurant supply firm:

"Don't Let Soggy Fries Dampen Your Profits!"

(And you thought you had problems.)

You get the idea. The headline must be clear and specific, it must get the reader's attention, and it must be a "me too" for the prospect. It doesn't always have to be a negative connotation, though. For example, when someone is considering our coaching and consulting services, we give them a copy of an article we wrote called "The Top Ten Questions to Ask Before Hiring a Coach." That headline is a "me too" primarily because if someone is considering hiring a coach they want to make an informed decision.

An important component to getting someone's attention is to always focus on what they are buying rather than on what you are selling. This is a huge distinction. Marketing experts constantly urge their clients to "stay on message" by hammering on their Unique Value Proposition (UVP). A UVP speaks to the primary benefit a customer or client locks in on when they examine your offer. Think about it. Bagged lettuce is very popular in grocery stores today. But what is it that people are really buying? They are buying a salad and they are buying time. People don't buy cell phones; they buy mobility and a sense of connectivity. It sounds counterintuitive when you think of how connected people are today with instant messaging and email. But they can feel in touch yet out of reach. Talking on a cell phone gives an even greater sense of belonging. Marketers understand that and their campaigns reflect this reality.

Apply the same mindset when sculpting a promotional campaign. As the saying goes, people don't buy a drill, they buy holes!

The I in AICA Stands for *Interest*

Once you have the reader's attention, you then want to hold their attention and build their interest. Consider what legendary marketing guru

David Ogilvie said: "You can't bore someone into buying something." Most marketing efforts are long-winded data dumps that aren't compelling. Keep this old marketing precept in mind: "Facts tell, stories sell."

The best way to shift a campaign from a "so what" to a "me too" is to tell a story that the reader can connect with or to paint a picture with a specific episode that the reader can relate to. Using our "Top Ten Questions to Ask Before Hiring a Coach" article as a further example, the opening paragraphs create a scene of a person who has decided to hire a coach but is uncertain about how to choose one. You can see the article on our website to understand the concept of building interest with this approach.

Another way to build interest is to use phraseology and sound bites that the prospective client can relate to. Here are a few examples that you can build on and customize to frame your points and ideas with:

- You might be saying to yourself...
- Don't you owe it to yourself...?
- Every once in a while, an opportunity comes along...
- A commonly asked question by our clients is...
- If you are like most (target market) we speak with, you...
- As someone who works closely with (target market)...

The C in AICA Stands for *Confidence*

Once you have people's attention and their interest builds, you have to strengthen their confidence to buy. The best way to do this is to use what is called social proof. People want to know what other people like them are saying as a result of taking action. Well-placed testimonials are perfect evidence. On our website, for example, there is a button that says, "Click to read and hear what our clients are saying." What your clients say about you is far more persuasive than anything you can say about yourself.

To prove our point on both targeting and social proof, here's a story of a guy we know who owns a window-washing firm that caters to wealthy homeowners. He started by selecting affluent neighborhoods and then offered to do a few homes with an introductory cut-rate offer. On the day that he was booked to perform the service, he would knock on the doors of the neighbors, pretending to be lost. The neighbor would answer the door and the window washer would greet him or her and say, "Sorry to bother you. I'm here to clean the Hendersons' windows. Do you know which house is theirs?" We're not kidding. And we're not suggesting you resort to trickery. This is simply to illustrate how the dominos can start falling as social proof gathers steam. This guy "owned" his neighborhoods in short order. After all, if he was good enough for the Hendersons…

The Last A in AICA Stands for *Action*

Always ask them to take action, but make it easy to opt in. Take the abstract of what you do down to something non-threatening, easy to conceptualize, and noncommittal, and differentiate it with value. Every single marketing effort should encourage a learning experience. Provide something value-added that people will actually find to be of value. Again, in our article, "The Top Ten Questions to Ask Before Hiring a Coach," we say right up front, "Whether or not you hire us is secondary at this point. Use this document as part of your due diligence process before you hire any coach or consultant and ask them these questions." And the article provides the list of questions. How valuable is that? It requires no commitment and the questions are absolutely essential for everyone to ask before hiring a coach.

GIVE THEM SOMETHING MEANINGFUL TO ASK FOR

Whatever your profession is, you can create a Top Ten Questions to Ask document. Then develop a call to action that encourages your prospective clients to ask for it. Remember, it is a call to ACTION. You want them to take action. Home Depot and other large firms have figured this out, albeit in a simplistic way. At an NHL hockey game we noticed that a large sign that normally read Home Depot was changed to read HomeDepot.Com. The sign was changed to tell people to do something rather than just saying, in essence, remember us?

Suppose a restaurant in a funky part of town decides to try to increase business by putting a neon sign in the window that says, "Get in here!" Sure enough, business will pick up. Tell people what you want them to do.

In a small enterprise, you can't just go through the motions. You see a lot of entrepreneurial markets that "waste" their calls to action. For example, you see a bus bench ad for a real estate agent. It looks like every other billboard ad for a real estate agent you've ever seen and probably has the same bland call to action every other agent uses—"Call for a free home evaluation." So what! (He'd be better off standing outside tearing up twenty-dollar bills on a windy day—he'd get the attention of more passing motorists with that technique than with the easy-to-dismiss ad.) What if the call to action read, "Call us to receive this report: The Top Ten Questions to Ask Before Buying a House in (your neighborhood)"? That is intriguing, unique and conveys a benefit.

The ideal call to action is one that provides a tangible benefit. A men's clothing store would be far better off advertising a sport jacket sale by saying, "Buy a sport jacket and receive a free pair of dress slacks" than saying, "All sport jackets are thirty percent off." It is easy to conceptualize a pair of free pants. It's also easy to dismiss a pseudo thirty percent off sale.

GIVE PROSPECTS A BRIDGE TO CROSS

On some occasions it is a good idea to delay gratification and offer something small to make it easy and non-threatening for prospective clients to opt in and respond to your promotional offer. People get so pounded with promotional materials these days that they often tune out everything without giving it a chance. This is especially true if your solutions are expensive or complex or if you have a substantial amount of competition.

Sometimes you need a "bridge" to help with the sifting of prospects from suspects. By this we mean that you make your call to action simple and easy to act on with little commitment necessary on the part of the prospective client. But it gets the process started.

For example, Disney Resorts will often promote their theme parks on television but rather than tell you to call them to book your vacation they will invite you to order a free DVD to learn about all the new and great things taking place at their properties. If you are sorta-kinda on the verge of thinking about maybe-perhaps starting to consider vacation options, that's a pretty non-threatening, non-committal way to begin. And here's our question: Are you more or less inclined to travel to one of their theme parks after you and your family watch the video? Heck, by simply receiving the video in the mail you become more predisposed to go.

Software firms offer free sampler programs or inexpensive "loss-leader" packages just to get you to opt in and contact them. Again, the conversion rate increases.

In both the Disney and software examples, there is another issue to consider: The firms are acquiring valuable names of prospective clients. This is called Predisposed Lead Acquisition (unfortunately it makes for a lousy acronym). Once they receive your contact information they will put you into a process and "DRIP" on you for all eternity. We'll talk more about DRIP marketing in a moment.

Here is one last example to consider. At our firm, we have expensive and complex coaching and consulting solutions and a few seemingly sophisticated technology solutions, as well. We say "seemingly" because, while not in reality, the optics with technology for many people is that they are complicated and esoteric. Couple that with the fact that with many of our prospective clients, we aren't creating a need. By that we mean that many of our prospective clients are currently using a competitor's solution and we are trying to break the status quo and urging them to consider their options—us.

The same is true for your business. People are busy and, unless they are completely disillusioned with their current provider, if the solution is "big and complicated," it's easy to put off until, well, never. The Law of Diminishing Intent strikes again.

To address this in our business, we created an inexpensive kit that gives people a sampling of actionable tools that prospective clients of ours can stress test without a big commitment of time or money. This $250 bridge lets people "raise their hands" and show interest and curiosity for us and test the waters. And it also gives us a steady stream of inbound calls from people who are, to varying degrees, predisposed.

Your job at this point is to consider how you can refine your calls to action to incorporate some of these time-tested precepts. The beautiful thing about this as well as the overall AICA and PAS methodology is that it can be applied to virtually all marketing efforts, so use it as a frame of reference going forward.

DRIP ON THEM

Okay, so you've identified your target market and you've created your campaign. Now what? You need to launch the campaign. You may be shocked to read this but we have yet another acronym for you. This one is DRIP, which stands for *discipline, respect, inform* and *persist*.

The concept of DRIP marketing has been around for a long time. Bill collectors have been using their own variations of spaced-repetition dripping for years. (Please don't ask us why we know this. It was a long time ago.) They send a sequential stream of several linked letters followed up by phone calls to "nudge" a delinquent customer into paying up. The science is that with every drip, the likelihood they will get paid increases. If you are serious about standing out from the pack and distancing yourself from your competitors, you have to be resigned to a campaign that includes DRIP marketing.

The D in DRIP Stands for *Discipline*

In all of your marketing efforts it is essential that you be *disciplined*. Be disciplined in your targeting. Be disciplined in your distribution. Don't get faked out into thinking, "More is more. I'll send out more."

We all get junk mail all the time from companies offering furnace cleaning, lawn care, and so on, and most of it is easy to dismiss and forget because it is sent "one-off." This means we receive it once and then probably never again. It was a company prospecting via a shot in the dark.

By using frequency in your distribution, you create familiarity and that positions you for when the recipient's stage of readiness kicks in. We would much rather you send a string of seven batches of five hundred direct mail pieces linked and sequentially tied to each other over a seven-month period than to send thirty-five hundred pieces one-off.

Each DRIP triggers a moment of recognition that builds confidence and trust. When you build AICA and PAS into each DRIP, you are putting the odds in your favor that eventually the prospective client will warm up to you.

The R in DRIP Stands for *Respect*

When you market to prospective clients, we suggest that you lean on them respectfully. Much of the DRIP marketing used today is annoying, which explains why we are not the biggest fans of cold-calling—it's not respectful. Think about all the cold calls you get. They are the ultimate disrespectful interruption. Do you really want to be in the same category? Be practical, be strategic, and ask yourself, "How does this reflect on us?"

Consider, too, if a new client is going to be swayed by a cold call, how much can you expect in terms of loyalty from this person? It's reasonable to think they can be easily lured away by a competitor who cold calls them down the road. Don't you really only want the kind of clients who slam the phone down when they get cold-called?

If you do want to reach out with a phone call, why not send a string of three linked and sequential direct mail pieces and then follow up with a phone call? This way you can point to the information in the three pieces and make your call to action a reinforcement of your offer.

The I in DRIP Stands for *Inform*

Coincidentally, the best way to be respectful is to bring as much value as possible. Teach prospective clients something they probably don't know about your sector. Offer meaningful information that they can translate into results. Our Top Ten Lists, for example, bring value that readers can use regardless of whether or not they do business with us. That is informative.

Also, look at how the word *form* exists within the word *inform*. Value-added content can include relevant information that goes beyond your message. If you are targeting business owners, for example, your value-added content can speak to their *occupation* as well as your *message*. Many good accountants provide value-added financial tips that their clients can relay to their kids—*family*. FORM can be a tremendous point of difference to help your prospecting efforts stand out from the pack.

Another way to make your efforts informative is to simply make the information you send easy to read and process. With letters, or any form of advertising, ensure it has a Dual Readership Path. What does this mean? Suppose you're at the airport and you're about to take a trip so you want to buy a magazine. You grab *Esquire* or *Vanity Fair* or whatever catches your eye. You don't necessarily buy it right off the bat; you stand there for a few minutes. You look at the cover to see if anything interests you and you flip through it to see if anything gets your attention. You see an article. Do you start reading it word for word? No. You do a panoramic scan of the article, looking at pictures, statements in bold font, and pull quotes. What are pull quotes? They're quotes pulled out of the article and sprinkled throughout it to engage your interest. You're interested, so you fold it up and pay for it. (You may have noticed that there are italicized comments, quotes and other features designed to break up the content of this book. This offers someone who is casually perusing it a chance to get a sense for the ideas and theme quickly.)

Use the same approach in all forms of your promotional efforts. Remember AICA. If we send you a letter, it'll have the introductory components, then it'll have a bold hook. We'll present a problem you can relate to. And then it'll have text. Between the first and second paragraph will be another bold statement, maybe to agitate the problem, and then another bit of text and then one more bold statement that makes a promise about our solution.

Problem, agitate, solve and then the call to action in the text. Here's the point. When you open the letter, do you start reading it word for word? No. You scan it. You'll look at the bold text and probably the P.S. at the bottom.

You may find it interesting to know that this approach speaks to both the left and right brain. Right brain people don't look for as much detail as left brain. The body of the text gives you detail. The words in bold get your attention. Use this in your emails, in your ads, whatever the case may be. (You can see sample letters on our website.)

The P in DRIP Stands for *Persist*

Be persistent, especially if you are narrowcasting and specializing in your prospecting efforts. There's an old saying that "If you're well-targeted, drip on them 'til they buy or die." It may take seven letters, it may take seventeen hits, before they actually opt in and engage. If it's well-targeted, what you're trying to do through "frequency and recency" is contrast yourself to their current provider, distance yourself from everybody else, and build a relationship of value because you're fast-tracking them to advocacy.

We don't mean to oversimplify prospecting by just glancing off some of these points. We want to give you some fundamentals. Are you targeted? Is there value? Are you hanging in there?

ADDITIONAL POINTS TO CONSIDER

In a few pages, we're going to outline some other prospecting methods for you to consider. For now, let us give you some more points to ponder regarding target marketing with direct mail and some essential ideas to apply when you actually meet with prospective clients for the first time.

- Start every letter you send with what is called a "'drop-down" letter—the first letter of the first word of the first paragraph is larger than the rest. Magazines do this all the time and it has been proven to make your letter more inviting to the reader.
- Ensure that the opening paragraph is brief and catchy. Again, like a good magazine article, you are trying to draw readers in early so that they will stay committed and read it through to the end.
- Be specific. Avoid talking in generalities. Stephen Covey didn't call his book *The Habits of Highly Effective People*. He offered the seven habits and instantly made the prospective book buyer think, "Seven? I can do seven." A classic me-too title.
- Clearly explain benefits. Telling isn't selling, as the old saying goes. Introduce a concept and then elaborate with vivid descriptions and engaging phraseology that the prospective client

can use to envision a payoff. The phrase "What this means to you..." is an ideal entree to a feature-benefit elaboration.

- Be conversational. Write a letter as if you were sending it to a good friend. Again, you aren't trying to impress anyone; you are trying to impress upon them that you can be trusted.

FOUR MARKETING "DON'TS"

The following are four mistakes that can undermine an entrepreneur's prospecting efforts:

- Don't data dump. Focus on your Unique Value Proposition and whet the prospective clients' appetite. Then leave them wanting more. Brevity is key. If they see that your promotion requires a large commitment of time to read, they will likely not even start.

- Don't spray and pray. We've already said it, but repeat it because this is a common mistake that small enterprise marketers make. Be diligent and focused—always.

- Don't bail. Former British Prime Minister Margaret Thatcher said it best: "It's easy to be a starter, but are you a sticker, too? It's easy enough to begin a job, but harder to see it through." That mantra is often what separates the best from the rest in virtually everything, including prospect target marketing.

- Don't ignore the numbers. You've heard it before—marketing is a numbers game. Everything is a numbers game. Golf is a numbers game. The card doesn't ask "how?" it asks "how many?" The little box for each hole is too small for an explanation; it's only big enough for a number. The bible is the most stolen book in North America. That seems counterintuitive, but look at the numbers. It is the most printed book in North America, so there's more opportunity to steal one. Numbers tell the whole story. The trouble is, most marketers pay little attention to the numbers. We're asking you to use even simplistic analytics to scrutinize your marketing efforts. Test a campaign on a small scale first to see how it plays out before you roll it out en masse. What is the opting in rate for prospects? At what point in the process do people convert from suspect to prospect? What is the conversion rate of prospects who opt in and then become customers or clients? You and your team have to analyze your numbers so that you can refine your efforts and then decide if you want to scale out the campaign to a larger extent. Think of marketing like a boomerang. You send it out and it should come back. What do you call a boomerang that doesn't come back? A stick! You send out some marketing materials, so some responses should come back. By knowing the numbers, you can make quantifiable improvements to your approach over a reasonable period of time.

THE MOMENT OF TRUTH: THE PROSPECT OPTS IN!

When your target marketing efforts sift out prospects from suspects and you start meeting with the people you attract, be certain to employ the consultative approach we discussed earlier in the book. Use an agenda, have no hidden agenda, and strive for fit based on your Triple-A Ideal Client Profile.

As we've said already, unless you are a transactional marketer—meaning a prospective client buys something from you but you may never see him or her again—we urge you to use stewardship rather than salesmanship. It's absolutely true that your persuasive impact will increase when you stop trying to sell to people. This is especially true with high-net-worth prospective clients. Affluent people, for the most part, don't like to or want to be sold to. The more you push them, the more you will repel them. They do, however, expect that you will try to sell to them when you meet them for the first time. It is a refreshing eye-opener for them when they realize that you are different. You automatically become more compelling and attractive.

Most salespeople look at the sales process as being linear, with the end point being the sale. The salesperson creates an emotional state in order to motivate a customer to satisfy a real or perceived need. Motivation is mistaken for trust in this process. Eighty percent of all effort is spent completing the process and making the "close," or the "sale," or "doing the deal." The customer is then left with a product that satisfied the emotional state at that moment, but because it was driven by external motivation (the salesperson's) rather than self-motivation (the customer's), a sense of buyer's remorse or anticlimax can appear. At the end of this process, the salesperson must look for a new sale to make, using the remaining twenty percent of his effort to get back in front of past customers. The treadmill continues from sale to sale.

Consultation is a dynamic cycle based on gaining permission to proceed with a proposed course of action. In order to be granted permission, the consultant seeks to understand a need and then brings professional insight to planning and arranging a solution.

Unlike the sales process, the consultation process invests eighty percent of effort into enhancing the relationship by validating and strengthening the mutually agreed upon partnership between client and consultant. Only twenty percent of effort is expended on agreeing to results. The consultant does not need to continually feed the emotional state of the client. In other words, consultants continue to increase the value of the relationship by demonstrating solutions rather than the need to purchase a product. The result is that the client becomes an advocate instead of remaining a client or customer. Advocates will bring more of their personal business to the consultant and will encourage others to seek the trusted services the consultant provides.

ADDITIONAL PROSPECTING CONCEPTS

The Telephone

We've stated our case regarding cold-calling. The phone is a powerful tool, but should be used as a complement to more respectful efforts to build a foundation of trust and familiarity with a prospective client. As we explained, if you were to send two or three sequential introductory letters to a prospective client first and then follow up and point to those letters, you've already propelled yourself above most of your competitors.

That said, there are exceptions to every rule. You may be a marketer who not only promotes a product or solution that is conducive to cold-calling but who is actually comfortable with the concept of cold-calling (one in a million). Again, we're not big fans of the concept, but if that describes your scenario, here are a couple of pointers to put the odds in your favor.

Always, in a relaxed and low-key manner, acknowledge the prospective client's time and immediately ask for permission to forward information that he or she can review prior to a future conversation.

> Good afternoon, (first name), don't mean to bother you, I know you must be busy. My name is (insert name here), and I was wondering if I could quickly introduce myself and get your permission to forward some information about all that we do for our clients, many of whom, like you, are (describe them).

This either-or approach, along with a relaxed tone, will quickly take you to a fork in the road. Either they will invite you to go ahead and the conversation will evolve, or they will decline. If positive, congruently stick with a consultative approach and build rapport. If you are rejected, take the high road.

I completely understand that now is not a good time. Would you mind if I periodically touched base with you in the future to update you on what we're doing for our clients and to forward information that could be of interest to you?

Again, you are at another fork in the road. Either you will be invited to stay in touch—by which the prospective client is admitting something very important to you—or you won't be. They might be saying, "No!", "Not Now!" or "I Don't Know!" The door might be open for you to contrast yourself to their current provider and eventually earn the right to discuss things in the future. If you are completely shut down, bow out gracefully and move on. Again, you are trying to find prospective clients, not create them. Sift prospects from suspects and build from there.

Seminars

For a number of our clients, seminars have been a reasonably good way to attract prospective clients within a captive environment and showcase their services. We also have a number of clients who no longer do seminars or refuse to go down this road altogether. As one client said to us, "I used to do seminars, but now I call them 'barbeques'—this way good people actually show up and bring friends with them." All things being equal, if you had a choice between doing either a Client Advisory Council or Client Appreciation event or a seminar for prospective clients, there is no question which we would suggest you do. If you wanted to do all of the above, good for you! Here are a few pointers:

- Keep the event small and intimate.
- Record it and create an executive summary for those who didn't attend. Send it as part of a "Did you miss it?" campaign for prospective clients to review and for clients to offer to friends and acquaintances.

- Assuming that the event is successful, create an ironclad process so that you can replicate the event in the future. The process, like a Client Advisory Council, involves three key components: the ramp-up for inviting people and logistics; the execution, where you actually conduct the event, and then the follow-up, where you convert prospects up the Loyalty Ladder.

- Master the art of presenting. Be scripted, use humor, get the audience engaged, and keep refining your approach—it is an art form. We love to hear great presenters in action. We had a client who would conduct seminars on tax and estate planning, and while the message was good, the messenger was lacking. He asked us for ideas on how he could improve the content. We informed him that the content was great, but that he needed to closely examine his presentation style. All we did was give him structure, ideas for handouts and scripting, and most of all, a direction for humor. He began to ask questions like "What is the difference between tax evasion and tax avoidance? About seven years …" After a while he became a master, and rather than dreading doing his speeches he couldn't wait to get in front of a microphone.

Trade Shows

Based purely on return on investment—both in terms of time and money—we're not the biggest fans of trade shows. But, like cold-calling, there are exceptions here.

As always, an event must be consistent with your target market so that you can see both clients and prospective clients at the event. To avoid swimming in that pool of sameness, add some personality to an event. As Warren Buffett said, "The marketplace will pay you more to entertain it than it will to educate it." Stand out by adding something attention-getting. We've had clients rent fly-fishing simulators, golf putting greens and/or net assemblies that people could drive golf balls into. It's inviting and enables you to break the ice. You become more approachable and it's definitely better than handing out wads of free shiny stuff like pens and calculators—the approach used by most of your competitors.

You have to remember that trade shows and free seminars tend to cater to the junkies—those who make it part of their purpose in life to attend as many of these free events as possible. You can spot them a mile away. They are the ones with the plastic bags full of free swag at trade shows and the ones eating all the free muffins at the back of the seminar room. Remember, you aren't in the "suspecting" business. You are prospecting to attract people who meet your Ideal Client Profile.

Print Advertising

Most newspaper and magazine ads are about as effective as billboard signs and bus bench advertisements. They say to the world, "Here I am," and that's about it. They're glorified business cards that an advertising sales rep sold to the business based on the merit of how many "impressions" the ad would receive. Impressions are their best guesstimates for how many people might see (ignore?) the ad during a given period. How truly valuable are impressions to your business? That and five dollars will get you a cappuccino. You can't meet payroll based on how many impressions you get. It's all about converting people up the Loyalty Ladder. Period. If you can't quantify the value of a marketing effort, then we would suggest you avoid it.

Yellow page ads and websites are essential for some small businesses, but again, don't just go through the motions. In both cases, have a strong hook that highlights your UVP, use social proof and have a great call to action.

We're reminded of a financial advisor client who ran yellow page ads that were essentially business cards. To defend himself he said, "But look, I have a valuable call to action in the ad." It read, "Call me to receive a complimentary review of your portfolio." To which we said, "How many people—approximately—have called you in the last twelve months saying, 'Hi, I just saw your ad in the phone book and I'd like to receive that complimentary review of my portfolio...'?" You know the answer. He altered his ad to offer a video of him introducing himself and outlining his asset management philosophy and him interviewing a fund analyst. The video was reasonably inexpensive to make and extremely popular. Not only did prospective clients ask for it, but he also used it as part of his "tell-a-friend" campaign with tremendous results. We urged him to send a package of microwave popcorn to all of the recipients just to add a little personality to the concept. That built great buzz and softened prospective clients dramatically to be more open to a follow-up conversation. As we said, minor adjustments can lead to major improvements.

SHIFTING GEARS

We've talked about strategic analysis, we've talked about targets and goals, and we've talked about actions in terms of which activities are the best use of your time—the activities you must engage in. We're hoping you'll go back to your existing clients and their prospective promotional partners, based on CAST (the Client Advisory Support Team concept), and stimulate enough new business in those areas to the point where prospecting is a bonus.

For most entrepreneurs, prospecting is the engine of their business. They spend so much time on new clients that they almost punish existing clients by neglecting them. Don't focus on gathering all these new relationships at the expense of your existing and potentially un-maximized relationships. If you have even one existing relationship with a client who hasn't been communicated with in terms of why/who/how regarding your refer-ability, they are nothing more than a dormant asset. It's like keeping money under the mattress or in a bank account that earns enough interest to barely keep up with inflation, rather than investing in a solid stock or mutual fund.

We'd much rather see your business thrive with three hundred advocates than watch you simply survive, working long hours, cycling through a thousand customers and clients.

Remember

All of your prospect target marketing efforts must be well-targeted and:

» get their ATTENTION— "me too" versus "so what"
» hold their INTEREST—facts tell, stories sell
» build their CONFIDENCE—use social proof
» ask for their ACTION—give them something to ask for

and

» present a PROBLEM they can relate to
» expand and AGITATE the problem
» offer a solid SOLUTION to the problem

and

» be DISCIPLINED
» be RESPECTFUL
» be INFORMATIVE
» be PERSISTENT

Take Action Now! (Week 12)

» Review the Target Marketing Checklist found on our website, **www.paretoplatform.com**, and use it to scrutinize your current prospecting efforts.
» Visit **www.breakthroughbusinessdevelopment.com** to see updates and insights from the field on this topic and others.

PART 4:
REALITY CHECK
(WEEK 12)

CHAPTER 14
HOLDING YOURSELF ACCOUNTABLE

If it is to be, it is up to me.

William H. Johnsen

O nce you've conducted your Strategic Analysis, established your Targets and Goals, and identified which activities you should engage in, all you need to do to finish the STAR process is conduct a personal Reality Check.

If you've gotten this far in our process, you are obviously serious about achieving a breakthrough in your business. The first question you have to ask yourself at this point is: *What kind of skills and qualities do I need to develop and refine in order to bring my plan to reality?* We are constantly asking our clients—and each other—that question. We never get tired of it because we are constantly evolving and challenging ourselves to achieve new heights.

Because of our fixation on execution, the beauty of holding yourself, and your team, accountable is that it reminds you that when it comes to achieving a breakthrough, it's all about results. This process will continually refocus you towards ongoing implementation of the strategies that matter most to your business. As we said in the beginning, the value of reading a book like this really begins when you are finished reading it, when you come to the point where you have to decide where to go from here. We'll say it again: After all is said and done, more is often said than done. What are you planning to get done going forward?

DON'T LET YOUR INTENT DIMINISH

We've seen how procrastination and the Law of Diminishing Intent can rob an entrepreneur of the quantifiable results that can come from implementing relevant strategies and concepts.

If we want things to change in our business, we have to change. It starts with leadership. We absolutely must be committed to self-development and refinement in order to attract the kind of clients and have the kind of business we want. A mentor once told us that income rarely exceeds self-development. Yes, formal education can get us a job and make us a living, but there's also limitless self-education. To earn more, we really must learn more, which explains why we are constantly reminding our clients (and ourselves) to be serious students.

THE QUALITIES OF SUCCESS

We all see books, CDs and websites talking about the secrets of success or new ideas. They're not secrets. They're not new, either, even though they might be new to you. It is all about proven skills. And the great thing is that all of the books have already been written and are waiting for us to read them. New ones come out all the time, but they're often rehashing or reframing what's already been said somewhere else. Thankfully, repetition is the mother of learning.

All we have to do is seek out the knowledge. Everything is a study. Marketing is a study. Practice management is a study. Business development is a study. Parenting is a study. Marriage is a study. Sure, some things are innate and they just come to us naturally. But anyone who says they have all the answers hasn't heard all the questions. Our results plateau when our knowledge and commitment to implementation plateaus.

It is for that reason that we have assembled a list of qualities we have found most top entrepreneurs possess and continually refine. We are fortunate in that we are continually exposed to businesspeople who are open enough to share their successes and setbacks. In our consultations with these people, they reveal—sometimes subtly—aspects of their philosophy for life and business. Over the years we've noticed some commonalities. We've packaged this list within the word *breakthrough*. Each letter represents a quality of success.

Obviously, this list does not address every quality, nor is it in any specific order. Admittedly, we got creative with our choice of words to fit them into our acronym, but hey, it's all in the name of packaging.

Examine how you are doing in these areas. While a lot of what follows is a recap of what we've covered leading up to now, it never hurts to hear it again.

B.R.E.A.K.T.H.R.O.U.G.H. TO THE NEXT LEVEL

Belief

Top entrepreneurs have an unshakeable belief in themselves. This quality produces two key elements to success: self-motivation and resilience. They don't need to be motivated externally very often (their kids and families take care of that); there is an internal fire that burns within that causes them to hustle their way to their goals. They know that external motivation can have the lasting value of a wind-up toy. Like a top athlete who strives to train harder than his or her competitors, top entrepreneurs pour it on. What drives them? Is it pure ambition, fear of failure or simply a desire, a desire to make an impact and to build something that is valuable and that they can be proud of?

They also know that adversity is indeed a better coach than success. When there are no trials, success has less value. We've seen entrepreneurs whose businesses had essentially flatlined. Ninety-nine percent of the world would have given up, but not these people. They knew that you only fail when you give up and quit. You can't fail if you never fold. Looking back, even we thought there was a hint of delusion involved, yet sure enough, through belief and resilience, these people are living the entrepreneurial dream, fully and completely. This brings to mind a Chinese proverb that says a diamond cannot be polished without friction, nor a man without trials.

Everyone faces adversity. The key is, will you overcome it or be overcome by it? Top athletes don't feel pressure, they apply it, meaning they don't let fear or negativity pile up and overtake their optimism and confidence in themselves. Belief protects your goals and insulates your thoughts from sliding into a pattern of unconscious negativity.

Throughout this book we have talked about several immutable laws. We all have to respect these laws. The Law of Gravity is a good example. It's doesn't matter how motivated, optimistic or hardworking we are, if we jump off a cliff, something very predictable is going to happen.

Some laws are a little more business-specific than others, and Murphy's Law is an interesting example. When designing a business plan, it is crucial that we temper our expectations to compensate for external dependencies or slight errors in judgment.

Now, on the surface there appears to be a contradiction here when you also consider the Law of Positive Expectation, which states that what we expect to happen often will happen, eventually. There is the key word—eventually. How many times have you to set out to achieve something and you did get there but it took longer than you planned? It's happened to all of us.

And this brings us right back to the Law of Attraction. We, like a lot of people, believe that your results are a manifestation of your thoughts. We believe you'll see it when you believe it.

Without a solid belief in what you are doing, you open yourself up to negativity. That negativity is a collection of thoughts that can manifest in you, attracting something you don't want. Focus on what you do want and protect that vision with an unshakeable belief that you will accomplish it.

Responsibility

When things go wrong, it's due to one of the following: misfortune or misconduct. Top entrepreneurs take full responsibility for everything that happens on their watch. They don't go looking for someone to blame when things go off track—they hold up the mirror to themselves. They don't wish for things to improve; they look for ways to improve themselves. It's often a business owner's decisions rather than market conditions that determine a level of achievement. Taking responsibility is the key to turning uncertainty into certainty —to transforming potential into actual results.

Empowering

Top entrepreneurs know that most limitations are self-imposed, meaning that a breakthrough often occurs through the selection and empowerment of a good team. They also understand that a major component of their personal legacy stems from investing themselves in others. There are few things more fulfilling in business than to have a long-term employee tell you that the best decision they ever made was coming on board with you. But like most things, this happens by choice, not by chance. There also needs to be a collaborative, empowering culture in place, where employees know they are valued.

Once you have a carefully selected team on board, systems, procedures and accountability must be put in place. Structure and organization liberates talent so that it can really flourish and creates an environment of perpetual learning and refinement. Confucius said it best: "Give a man a fish and you feed him for a day. Teach a man to fish and you feed him for a lifetime." He also said, "When the student is ready, the teacher will appear." You must be patient to let certain skills and qualities emerge in others naturally. We've all seen all-star, can't-miss rookie athletes take four or more years to blossom and break out. With systems and structures in place in your business, you can afford to be patient.

And keep in mind, people are watching—your kids, your staff, everyone. People learn more from how we conduct ourselves than from what we say. (If you want to get a kid to start reading, you can either tell them to read or you can be certain they catch you reading often.) Here is a simple list of questions to serve as gentle reminders about your mindset and decorum regarding leadership that will breed empowerment:

- Do you radiate a sense of speed and urgency?
- Are you calm in times of turbulence?

- Are you notably and sincerely kind to service people, such as waiters and cab drivers?
- Do you eliminate fear and intimidation in the workplace?
- Do you take responsibility for setbacks and give praise for breakthroughs?
- Do you disguise orders as suggestions?
- Do you comment on mistakes rather than criticize people?
- Do you continually empower people to see what it will reveal in them?

Top entrepreneurs do not take their frustrations out on their people. Most mistakes are honest and minor. Good people don't need to be berated to feel even guiltier than they already do. The only reason some people place blame (which disempowers others) is because it takes the focus off them and makes them feel better about themselves—short-term benefits that can and will fester into big time problems.

Be a serial question asker. As Socrates said, "Questions are the answer." People would come to him with questions and problems looking for answers. Socrates would reframe the questions and force the other person to think things through. Often people would come to their own conclusions, with a little steering, and feel empowered rather than feeling preached to.

And that brings us to the next thing we believe leads to success.

Asking

Top entrepreneurs are tremendous communicators with incredible persuasive impact. Whether it's in an encounter with a prospective client, presenting to an audience or simply rekindling staff motivation, the key to prompting others to take action is to be mindful of *how* you ask people to take action and *why*.

Preparation is paramount in all forms of communication. The old saying "Change your audience, not your message" simply reminds us that we have to be well-prepared for all scenarios that involve our persuasive abilities. Ironically, this preparation enables you to be more spontaneous and relaxed in such scenarios. You're not grasping for a question to ask, you are rehearsed and organized.

As we mentioned earlier, in all meetings you must have an agenda to give order and structure to the meeting. You must also enter into the meeting with a mindset we call ACE—yet (yawn) another acronym. *Ask* people for their advice and opinions, pay sincere *compliments* and *encourage* them to express and elaborate.

Below are some questions that fit within the ACE parameters.

- What criteria do you use to select a provider (in your business sector)?
- Why are you considering making a move to someone new?
- What would you like to see improved in this type of relationship?
- What would an ideal outcome look like to you?

Good questions engage the audience and naturally attract them to you. A good lawyer will tell you that if, during a trial, the judge isn't taking notes, he or she probably isn't engaged in the argument. Ask good questions and you'll get good answers that help lead your audience to his or her own conclusions, which will be, more often than not, mutually beneficial.

Knowledge

Top entrepreneurs understand the Law of Attraction. They know that they make themselves more attractive to the marketplace by constantly learning more, refining themselves and their habits. We are by-products of our habits and rituals—good and bad. As Warren Buffett said, "The chains of habit are too light to be felt until they are too heavy to be broken." That speaks volumes about both starting and breaking habits, doesn't it?

We've said before that in order to make ourselves more attractive to the marketplace, we have to study the necessary skills and implement them where relevant, and then make those actions habitual. Everything is a study. If a client of ours expresses to us that he or she is having problems in a certain area, one of the first things we will ask is "How many books have you read on this topic?" We don't mean to come off as sounding preachy, but every skill is a study and a book has been written to help refine every skill we want to improve. (Of course, the book we buy but don't read won't help much. We all can admit to buying a book and hoping that somehow just by holding it—through osmosis—things would get better. Although we do feel smarter because we own them.)

But knowledge obviously goes beyond books. As Mark Twain said, "Don't let your schooling get in the way of your education." Experience is the ultimate teacher. Some things you can't learn in a simulator, for lack of a better analogy. Some people say that owning a dog is good practice for soon-to-be parents. As parents we can safely say that actually being a parent is the best teacher. As Sheryl Crow said, "You don't change diapers, they change you." A combination of reading and study, along with observation of others and personal experience, can lead to being enlightened in any area.

The continual quest for knowledge forces you to look at yourself and your approach. This personal analysis prompts you to consider what is in your enlightened self-interest. Knowledge of self is essential. It is important to remember that in business we have to strive to make a profit and leave a profit. But we can't do things at our own expense. Take time off. Do the things you want to do. Take impeccable care of those around you by taking impeccable care of yourself. Don't put off things until everything is in place or the circumstances are perfect. Pursue your goals—personal and business—in tandem.

Time Management

This is basically a misnomer, because you can't really manage time. So why call it time management? The clock moves forward relentlessly no matter what you do about it. You can, however, manage how you use your time and how we manage our activities and priorities.

Top entrepreneurs know that time is more valuable than money. You can earn more money but not so with time. So again, you have focus on what you get paid to do and create an array of processes for your team so that they can do what they get paid to do. This enables you to essentially "buy time." You can't make more, so buy some. You buy a power screwdriver for that reason. Why not do the same in your business?

Ironically, some entrepreneurs will claim to be too busy to put our processes into place. That is a classic chicken-and-egg scenario. Everyone is busy. What's interesting is that a struggling entrepreneur and an outrageously successful entrepreneur are both likely to tell you they are busy. But busy doing what? While we admire hard work, there are diminishing returns if you are mistaking motion for action. You have to focus on what matters most. Think of golf as an example. A decent golfer spends only about ninety seconds in a four-hour round actually hitting the ball. He or she might spend a total of thirty minutes addressing the ball and getting mentally and physically set to hit each shot. And, of course, the rest of the time is spent walking from shot to shot. We're not trivializing the importance of the mental focus and visualization that happens as he or she walks between shots, nor are we trivializing the importance of properly getting set before striking the ball. But the critical moments on the course are when the ball is actually hit.

In your business day, you have critical moments and then everything else. Everything matters and everything affects everything else. But some things matter more. Focus on those activities. No matter how busy you are, you must continually strive to achieve mastery in the areas that will most greatly affect your business.

It's like when someone once told us that they would like to write a book but couldn't find the time. We said, "Bill Gates wrote a book. Something tells us he's a little busier than you." Gives credence to the old saying "If you want something done, give it to a busy person."

Humility

It is incredibly impressive to meet people who have achieved immense success, yet don't take themselves too seriously or think they are any more special than the next person.

We've all experienced the antithesis of this—people who have a sense of self-importance that is downright painful. They should keep things in perspective. Sir Edmund Hillary does not have a picture of himself on the top of Mt. Everest. When he and Tenzing Norgay reached the summit, Hillary took a picture of his companion and then suggested they descend before an imminent storm blew in. He is humble and understated about his own accomplishments, yet excited to talk about the achievements of others.

If you've ever flown from New York City to Toronto, you may have had the opportunity to fly directly over Niagara Falls. Up close, the falls are an awesome and impressive sight to behold. But from twenty thousand feet, contrasted against the expanse of New York State and Ontario, the falls look like a leaky faucet dripping into a small sink. That's a metaphor we should all consider, no matter what level of success we achieve in business.

Success reveals a lack of humility in some people. We remember friends who, during the dot-com boom, attributed their (short-lived) financial breakthroughs to their own enlightened financial prowess. Their success was somewhat artificial, though, as it was achieved more from riding a wave than actual talent. It reminds us of the saying "Even turkeys can fly in a strong wind." But what's interesting is what happened when things unraveled. They pointed fingers and blamed circumstances. We don't wish anything less than success for anyone—we don't revel in anyone's personal setbacks. But we do appreciate when someone is humble and understated.

Reciprocity

Giving starts the receiving process. That is one heck of a powerful mantra to live by. The Law of Reciprocity reminds us that the world is round and things often come full circle. An entrepreneur who understands this is really putting the odds in his or her favor in terms of fulfillment and results.

This mindset reveals the personal agenda of the person on the receiving end. For those who respond to your "gift," you are attracting yet another person into your inner circle who is like-minded, and that brings good things out in you.

The Law of Environment states that we are products of our environment. The person you are becoming is so dramatically influenced by the people you are around, that we urge our clients to be hypersensitive about who they work, collaborate and network with. When you have a reciprocal mindset you attract others with a similar mindset. Over time you create a network of like-minded people who are always on the lookout for each other.

Entrepreneurs often work in isolation. In this era of independence, every now and again we need the mid-course correction that comes from bouncing ideas off someone who you can trust. We can't always believe our own hype. As Will Rogers said, "It's not what we don't know that causes us problems. It's what we know that ain't so."

Sometimes when we "pay it forward" there is no response or return. Like standing in a cavern with nothing but the sound of water dripping, you realize you're alone at that moment. That's fine. It doesn't affect your Karma in any way. You've put it out there and you benefit for that reason.

On Purpose

Our favorite clients over the years are people who do things on purpose. They are not at the mercy of external dependencies—the winds that blow. Instead, they have a plan and a personal sense of purpose—the set of the sail. Business owners who are deliberate and have a sense of purpose—meaning they feel that what they do matters—tend to achieve the best results over the long haul and realize a greater sense of fulfillment from their businesses. They also tend to bounce back from setbacks more quickly. Interestingly, the Japanese word for optimism literally means, having enough challenges to give life meaning and purpose. A sense of purpose can help you see stumbles for what they really are, stepping stones!

We can remember a financial advisor client who, when asked about his sense of purpose, told us, "I help people put their kids through college. I help people plan for a secure future. I help people make informed decisions to insulate themselves from things out of their control. I help clients transition their wealth and strengthen their legacy in the process. I love what I do." This is a guy who was slow out of the gate, took heat from his managers for being "too selective and methodical," yet eventually hit his stride and achieved tremendous success. Clients would move away from his city but want to keep him as their advisor. He had third-generation clients. It's no wonder why this advisor is in a league of his own today.

Urgency

Top business people have a sense of urgency when it comes to getting things done. Ironically, though, these same people can be patient and realistic about when real results will manifest—they just don't wait for conditions to be "perfect." They know that done is better than perfect and they focus on making things right as they go along. Is there a perfect time to have kids? Is there a perfect time to start investing in the stock market? Successful people in business believe that there has never been a better time to do something than *right now*. Having a sense of speed and urgency, along with a well-formulated approach in terms of activity, will add predictability to productivity.

Gratitude

Top entrepreneurs are often among the most gracious and appreciative people one can ever meet. This probably stems from the fact that they know how much work goes into achieving any kind of success. But they also remember the people who helped them along the way, as well as the people who weren't so fortunate. Not to get too cosmic, but the stars do have to align and they don't always seem to align for everyone, regardless of the effort that went into things. Again, there is the issue of misfortune and misconduct and for some people, no matter how hard they try, things don't seem to play out.

Top people have a profound respect for the fact that it takes everyone to make a community. Just as the African expression says "It takes a village to raise a child," it takes people of all kinds to create a culture and environment for success. Being mindful of that, not to mention grateful for our good fortune, is a common thread we see among top performers.

Honesty

The entrepreneurs we admire the most are the ones with unwavering integrity. They are authentic in their convictions and they strive to succeed through service to others, never at the expense of others. They have a code of conduct that insists that they deal with others honestly—and they are true to themselves.

So there you have it, qualities that enable business owners to achieve a breakthrough. Yes, we forced a few of these points to fit into our acronym—we know. But even so, the big question still comes back to you. At this stage of this book, have you started thinking about what you are going to do? We'll say it again: The value of this book begins right now. What are you going to implement? Sure, there is a lot of information packed into these pages—it's like taking the proverbial sip of water from a raging fire hose—but what will you take from this?

It's one thing to think about what you *should* do, but it's entirely another to focus on what you *will* do. Truthfully, we are not too concerned about how many books we sell (although a lot would be nice). We are concerned with the impact we have on business owners and the results they achieve. We know that sounds lofty and idealistic, but we really do care about implementation and results. As Ben Franklin said, "A sundial in the shade is wasted."

Let us ask you this: How close today are you to the goals you set for yourself five years ago? Looking back, does your life today closely resemble what you had in mind? Looking forward, where do you see yourself in the next five years? And what are you going to do to make that vision a reality?

What are you prepared to do differently? What are you prepared to do right now? What refinements are you going to make? Start with even just one idea before the Law of Diminishing Intent kicks in. Will you use an agenda in all of your meetings? Will you start doing call rotations? Perhaps a Client Advisory Council would be a good place to start.

If you could do only one thing, what would it be? One thing. If the one thing you did was sit down with your people and explain the Loyalty Ladder and the concept of advocacy and buying into something instead of buying something, this would be a good use of your time. If you called fifty Triple-A clients, incorporating FORM, and your team called two hundred other clients as part of the call rotation, that alone would make a difference. If the one thing you did was use an agenda in all of your meetings, this too would be a good use of your time.

What does it take to move forward with a new plan, to make sure nothing stands in the way of your success? Very simply, it is imperative that you take action right away. It doesn't matter what you do to forge ahead. It only matters that you make sure you do something to get the ball rolling. The sooner you put your plans into action, the more likely you are to achieve your goals.

ALL SYSTEMS GO!

One of the most important changes you can make is to adopt a systems-based approach to your business. Every process and activity you and your team execute on a daily basis must be planned, scripted, rehearsed, refined and well-documented in a Procedures Manual. Before you dismiss this as tedious, consider two key reasons why you should script your business from top to bottom:

1. Until your methodology is documented, it is not an intellectual property or asset.

2. If you don't document everything, chances are your business won't run smoothly unless you are there.

Systems ensure you aren't at the mercy of talent alone when it comes to your support staff. Our lawyer's business is held together by his legal assistant. He recently said, "Every time she returns from holiday, I have to give her a raise because she can see how the business nearly caved in without her."

Don't rely on maverick talent. Develop talent by creating a systematic approach you can hand to anyone to implement. You are truly on the verge of greatness when you have made yourself obsolete. Strive for the day when your business can run like a Swiss watch without you being there all the time. It's not only liberating, it's rejuvenating, and it drives the value of your business higher.

The primary benefits of a systems-based operating approach are improved predictability and efficiency. Your Procedures Manual serves as a Global Positioning System device guiding you and your team along the journey with precision. Without this approach, it would be like walking through uncharted territory at night with only a flashlight. A good plan, driven by systems, is like a beacon guiding you, drawing you in. It lets you see past short-term obstacles without the risk of drifting off course.

You've given a lot to your business, and it's time to get something back. Increased efficiency leads to more free time and you'll be able to recharge your batteries and balance your life.

This journey won't be without trials and frustrations. Shifting to an operational approach requires patience while it gains traction. It will require constant tinkering as you find the right mix of processes. But think about it this way: Is it only us who can't believe how fast time flies by? Look at how fast the last ninety days blew by. The next ninety could be even faster. Our point is that you could have much or all of what we've passed along put into place by then. What would that mean to you?

Think of exercise. If you did forty push-ups right now, the last five or ten would contribute most to building strength. However, the first thirty were necessary before you could get to the last ten and feel a benefit. You've probably already done the first thirty in your business just by starting your business, surviving (or thriving) for this long, while developing your skills and industry-specific knowledge. Finish the job and take your business to the next level by making the adjustments to your business that are certain to add quantifiable impact. Your confidence and interest in your business, not to mention your sense of fulfillment, will be stronger than ever.

Thank you for taking the time to read and consider our advice and opinions. It means a lot to us. Contact us with any questions you have or with your hero stories—we'd love to hear about them. Until then, best of luck in your pursuit of a breakthrough!

Remember

» Drive yourself and in the process you will drive systems, drive sales and drive results.

Take Action Now! (Week 12)

» Review the Accountability Worksheets found on our website, **www.paretoplatform.com**, to begin the process of translating these ideas into measurable results.

» Visit **www.breakthroughbusinessdevelopment.com** to see updates and insights from the field on this topic and others.

ACTIONABLE TEMPLATES ARCHIVED ON WWW. PARETOPLATFORM.COM

Week 1:
- STAR Business Planning Tool (ongoing)
- Sample Organizational Chart

Weeks 2 & 3:
- Sample Procedures Manual Menu
- Triple-A Ideal Client Profile Tool

Week 4:
- Sample FORM Client Profiling Tool
- Goal-Setting Worksheets

Week 5:
- Sample Service Matrix
- Sample Call Rotation Scripting

Week 6:
- Sample Client Advisory Council Campaign
- Sample Agendas

Week 7:
- Sample Customer Conversion Tool

Week 8:
- Sample Advocate Process

Week 9:
- Sample Referral Scripting

Week 10:
- CAST Strategic Alliance Scripting

Week 11:
- Client Milestone and Moment-of-Truth Guidelines

Week 12:
- Target Marketing Checklist
- Sample Action Planning Accountability Worksheets

ABOUT PARETO SYSTEMS CUSTOMIZED COACHING AND CONSULTING SERVICES

HAVE YOU HIT A PLATEAU WITH YOUR BUSINESS?

Pareto Systems and 8020Platform co-founders Duncan MacPherson and David Miller lead a team of dedicated business development and practice management consultants who help individual entrepreneurs translate ideas and concepts into results.

Their time-tested curriculum of actionable solutions can be sequentially deployed in a turnkey fashion. You will be able identify and capitalize on untapped opportunities that exist within your business and create a blueprint of proven strategies. Your personal coach will hold you and your team accountable as you embark on the step-by-step implementation process, which includes:

- how to competitor-proof your clients using a service matrix
- how to create consistency and build trusting client relationships
- how to fully capitalize on the Pareto Principle (80/20 Rule)
- how to attract a higher quality and quantity of referrals
- how to deploy predictable and sustainable systems

Our Diagnostic Assessment Process helps you and us determine if we are a good fit for each other. Contact us at 866.593.8020 to set up an introductory phone meeting.

Visit **www.paretosystems.com** to read "The Top Ten Questions to Ask Before Hiring a Coach." While you are there, you can also learn more about our:

- speaking engagements
- corporate consulting solutions
- content licensing and private label services
- management train-the-trainer programs.

PARETO PLATFORM SPOTLIGHT

Pareto Systems and Pareto Platform co-founders Duncan MacPherson and David Miller have created a Web-based business development and practice management dashboard that can quickly and efficiently propel your business to new heights.

This on-demand solution is available on a monthly subscription basis and is accessible 24/7. It is designed to enable you and your team to methodically implement our actionable concepts.

PARETO PLATFORM—
PROVEN STRATEGIES FROM $45.00 MONTHLY

Our entry-level Internet-based system gives you and your team 24/7 access to our time-tested business-building strategies with ongoing updates. Your personalized dashboard also provides you with a:

- customizable Organizational Chart
- personalized Procedures Manual
- Client Service Matrix
- Advocate Process

PARETO PLATFORM—
CLIENT RELATIONSHIP MANAGER (CRM)
FROM $95.00 MONTHLY

Our flagship solution gives you all of the great practice management and business development functionality found in the proven strategies version AND is fully integrated on a robust Client Relationship Management platform. This one-of-a-kind turnkey solution is all you and your team need to manage client relationships and run your business with precision and predictability. In addition, you will receive:

- Triple-A client relationship journals
- FORM client chemistry system
- full array of automated processes
- milestone recognition and DART deployment
- remote access and team oversight features

Visit **www.paretoplatform.com** for demo information and special trial offers.

A CALL TO ACTION FOR COACHES

Are you currently a practice management, business development or personal performance coach for entrepreneurs? Do you strive to become one in the near future? If so, Pareto Platform invites you to apply to become a certified and licensed coach to support entrepreneurs in your area in their quest to translate our proven strategies into results.

As a Pareto Certified Coach, you will receive:

- extensive training to gain mastery of all our strategies and procedures
- ongoing support from our VP of Consulting, Tom Frisby

- promotional support on our blog and website
- a full suite of tools to manage your business
- turnkey, actionable tools for every client you serve

To learn more, please visit **www.paretoplatform.com**.

LOOKING FOR HELP WITH IMPLEMENTATION?

LET THE PARETO PLATFORM TEAM HELP YOU IMPLEMENT ALL SEVENTEEN ACTIONABLE STRATEGIES IN THIS BOOK USING OUR VIRTUAL BOOTCAMP!

If you feel strongly about the concepts contained in this book but feel that you need assistance translating our ideas into results, sign up for our Virtual Boot Camp. This one-of-a-kind turnkey business building and practice management process is guaranteed to fast-track you and your team to success. By implementing our concepts, you are guaranteed to:

- Attract at least five new high quality referrals in the next ninety days
- Deploy a process to consistently attract high-caliber clients
- Run a far more precise and efficient business

Our sequential process consists of four live webcasts featuring Duncan and David walking you through our time-tested curriculum. You will be shown how to execute all seventeen actionable proven strategies—the same strategies our clients regularly pay in excess of $15,000 to learn through our one-on-one coaching program.

In addition, as you progress through our virtual boot camp, you will also receive unlimited access to our complete Pareto Platform dashboard, loaded with our business building tools during the ninety-day period. Your user name and password will enable you to tap into our complete array of scripts, letters, campaigns and templates. You will also receive unlimited ongoing access to our constantly updated weblog at **www.breakthoughbusinessdevelopment.com**.

So don't delay. If you want to make this year your best year ever, let Duncan, David and their team help you take your business to the next level.

Your investment is $495 and about two hours per week of learning and implementation. You and your entire team will receive full access to this program and it is fully guaranteed. If upon completion you are not completely delighted with your degree of implementation and results, we will promptly refund your investment.

Contact us at: 866.593.8020.

INDEX